WITH
GOD
on the GOLF
COURSE

Phil Callaway

HARVEST HOUSE™ PUBLISHERS

EUGENE, OREGON

Unless otherwise indicated, all Scripture quotations are taken from the *Holy Bible*, New Living Translation, copyright ©1996. Used by permission of Tyndale House Publishers, Inc., Wheaton, Illinois 60189, U.S.A. All rights reserved.

Verses marked NIV are taken from the Holy Bible: New International Version®. NIV®. Copyright © 1973, 1978, 1984 by the International Bible Society. Used by permission of Zondervan Publishing House. The "NIV" and "New International Version" trademarks are registered in the United States Patent and Trademark Office by International Bible Society.

Verses marked THE MESSAGE are taken from The Message. Copyright © by Eugene H. Peterson 1993, 1994, 1995. Used by permission of NavPress Publishing Group. All rights reserved.

Cover by Paz Design Group, Salem, Oregon

Backcover author photo by Jeffrey Callaway

WITH GOD ON THE GOLF COURSE
Copyright © 2002 by Phil Callaway
Published by Harvest House Publishers
Eugene, Oregon 97402
www.harvesthousepublishers.com

Library of Congress Cataloging-in-Publication Data
Callaway, Phil, 1961.
    With God on the golf course / Phil Callaway.
        p. cm.
    ISBN-13: 978-0-7369-0914-3
    ISBN-10: 0-7369-0914-1 (pbk.)

    1. Golfers—Religious life.   2. Golf—Religious aspects—Christianity.
  I. Title
    BV4596.G64 C35 2002
    242'.68—dc21   2002005632

All rights reserved. No part of this publication may be reproduced, stored in a retrieval system, or transmitted in any form or by any means—electronic, mechanical, digital, photocopy, recording, or any other—except for brief quotations in printed reviews, without the prior permission of the publisher.

Printed in the United States of America.

07 08 09 / BP-MS / 10 9 8 7 6

To my golfing buddies:
Vance, James, Ron, Dan, Mike, Sigmund, Gord, and Lauren—
in the hope that one day soon all of them will let me win.

Contents

A Note from Phil

Golf is a marvelous and maddening game that combines three favorite pastimes from my childhood: doing poorly at mathematics, taking long walks to get away from people, and hitting things with a stick.

Not everyone loves golf, though. John Wayne gave it up out of frustration, I'm told. It's amazing that a man who drew a six-shooter with lightning speed, won the battle of Iwo Jima almost single-handedly, and recaptured Bataan could be defeated by a 4-inch hole in the ground. But he was.

Columnist Westbrook Pegler was too. He once dubbed golf "the most useless game ever devised to waste the time and try the spirit of man." Once, after shanking five balls into a murky creek, I tended to agree with him. But mostly I've found the opposite to be true—golf is a useful game that teaches us more about life and faith than we think, if only we will listen.

This isn't a book about the mechanics of golf. Thousands of them already exist. This is a book about life. What follows are 32 short devotionals from one who is learning to pay attention to life and listen to God.

It's my prayer that the reading of this small book will heighten your enjoyment of this great game and, more importantly, increase your longing after God, the Master who promises to walk with us on every path our lives take—yes, even on the golf course!

Thanks for joining me. I wish we could talk about these things on a golf course somewhere, but until that happens, this book will have to do.

—Phil Callaway
Alberta, Canada

Come to me with your ears wide open.
Listen, for the life of your soul is at stake.
Isaiah 55:3

1

The Lost Art of Listening

"Many times God speaks to us through the things we love to do: sports, hobbies, work, and friendships. As a professional golfer, I am often asked for tips or advice. So here it is: Listen to what God can say to you through the game of golf."

—TOM LEHMAN

A few people have asked how I can write a devotional book based on a cruel sport that often rewards perseverance, courage, and devotion with ulcers. One person went so far as to say that it's tough to imagine Rembrandt or Mozart or King David being any good at this game. And he was probably right. But as I walk the course I realize that golf reflects life in a thousand ways.

Near the small town where I live, you can golf all year around by paying a mere $270 fee. Not that you'd want to. In December it's colder than a polar bear's kiss here, and by January the only people on the course are ice fishermen who sit around fires shivering and dreaming of August. But for three fabulous months of summer, there's nothing finer than an early morning walk down our narrow fairways, avoiding creeks teeming with catfish and sharing the fairway with tame deer who have been known to stroll over and check our scorecards.

Evenings bring postcard sunsets and a magical mist that blankets the greens, tucking them in until morning. I've golfed some of the finest courses in America, from Oregon's coast to Georgia's humidity, but none quite measure up to this nine-hole marvel near home. Here I learned to golf. And in learning to golf, I am discovering something far more important than the game itself.

I live a rather hurried life—nurturing a marriage, being a dad to three teenagers, speaking to groups 100 times a year, editing a magazine, writing books, and taking out the garbage. The golf course is one place where it's virtually impossible for me not to slow down, to find solitude, and to listen. I've listened to the advice of friends here, the struggles of my children, the counsel of my wife. And best of all, I'm learning to listen to God.

Not always. There are divots to replace, bunkers to traverse, frustrations to be taken out. I'm easily distracted. But for the most part, golf courses celebrate the virtue of silence, providing havens of stillness and solitude—welcome contradictions in a busy world. The first time I took my son golfing, he clapped as I chipped and cheered as I putted. It was tough explaining to him that *stillness* is rule number one in golf.

I need such a place, don't you? I am convinced that few things are more important today than stillness, because it is here that we learn to listen. Nothing about the world makes us want to listen, does it? We live in an increasingly noisy place where hurry and speed are the measure of a productive life. Isaiah 30:15 provides a wonderful contrast: "In quietness and confidence is your strength."

From start to finish, God's Word emphasizes the need to *listen*. Adam and Eve refused God's counsel and were banished from the Garden Golf and Country Club. Despite God's incredible blessing, Amaziah, king of Judah, turned to idols then watched his enemies break down Jerusalem's walls, raid the palace treasury, and take hostages. The reason? Amaziah would not listen to God's counsel either (2 Chronicles 25:16).

I, too, find it hard to listen. Once I golfed with a pro who, when I asked him, told me several things I was doing wrong (this took awhile). I nodded my head politely when he spoke. I smiled. But I was too proud to hear him. Listening, I have since discovered, is not the same as waiting your turn to speak or defend yourself.

In Jesus' letters to the seven churches in Revelation, it's significant that He closed all seven this way: "He who has an ear, let him hear what the Spirit says to the churches" (Revelation 2–3).

God honors those who listen. When the prophet Nathan confronted King David with his awful sins of adultery and murder, David listened. And he was called a man "after God's own heart."

God is still looking for a few good listeners, but we must have attentive hearts to hear what He is saying. May the stillness of a golf course remind us that often it takes less courage to stand up and speak than to sit down and listen.

⛳

Lord, help me have a heart that longs to hear Your voice.
One that is soft and teachable. Keep me from the distractions
of a noisy culture. Give me the wisdom to listen
to Your words—and obey. Amen.

Don't worry about anything; instead, pray about everything. Tell God what you need, and thank him for all he has done. If you do this, you will experience God's peace.
Philippians 4:6-7

2

Golf Light

"If there is a ball on the green and one in the bunker, mine is in the bunker."
—VANCE NEUDORF

You may remember the moment. Ian Woosnam sure does. He began the final round of the 2001 British Open in the lead. But after nearly acing the opening hole, the Welshman was informed by his caddie that they had 15 clubs in the bag—one more than the legal limit. Knowing the crime carried a two-stroke penalty, Woosnam almost had a stroke himself. He fired his hat to the ground, grabbed the offending driver, and hurled it from the tee box.

"I didn't really get it out of my head all the way around," Woosnam said later. "Everything seemed to be going against me." Haunted by the costly mistake, Woosnam bogeyed the next two holes and was four strokes off the mark when David Duval peeled off his sunglasses to accept the trophy.

Reminds me of another golfer I know. Me. I'm guilty of taking along extras. I've got the full set, plus a driving iron. I've got an oversized 1-wood named Bertha and a ball retriever in case she misfires. My pockets are heavy with coins and ball markers and tees and car keys. The mosquitos where I live show up on radar screens, so I throw in a generous bottle of repellant. And sunscreen. And Band-Aids. One can't be overprepared, so I bring along bottled water, aspirin, and a knife that doubles as a club head cleaner, a cleat tightener, a bottle-top remover, and an alarm clock. I keep an extra jacket in my bag, too. Rain pants. An umbrella. Club head covers. And a coupon book that expired last September.

Lugging all these accessories around the course made the rounds miserable, so I bought a small pull-cart to help me. Now I have a place to carry two more pop cans, the scorecard, four tees, and some extra pencils. If this continues, I'll have to buy another cart.

I know what you're thinking. *He's crazy. No one can enjoy golf with all that baggage.* And you're right. But let me ask you something. Have you done the same lately? I don't mean on the golf course. I mean in life. When you picked up the newspaper this morning, did you also pick up a load of fear and throw it in your bag? When you tucked your children in last night, or talked to the grandkids, did you shoulder a bag full of worries about the future? When you arrived at work, what was waiting there? Fatigue? Discouragement? Dissatisfaction? Anger? Fear? Did you pick them up? Did you throw them in your bag and lug them around all day?

If so, you may have discovered that it's impossible to experience the joyful life God intends when you carry concerns you were not meant to bear. In my experience, more people carry around the baggage of worry than all other addictions combined. Worry is an expensive habit and a club we cannot afford to carry. Like a rocking chair, it gives us something to do, but it won't take us anywhere. Worry forces us to live life burdened, missing the blessings around us and squinting at the unknown.

Listen to these liberating words of Jesus from Matthew 6:34: "Give your entire attention to what God is doing right now...and don't get worked up about what may or may not happen tomorrow. God will help you deal with whatever hard things come up when the time comes" (THE MESSAGE).

Scottish writer George MacDonald once said, "No man ever sank under the burden of the day. It is when tomorrow's burden is added to the burden of today that the weight is more than a man can bear. Never load yourself so."

What extras are you carrying in your bag today? Accept a little advice from Ian Woosnam and me: Take them out and lay them down before it's too late.

⚑

Dear Lord, You know what I've been carrying lately.
You know I'm weary from the weight. So I place my guilt,
anger, fear, and worry at Your feet.
Help me leave tomorrow's problems for tomorrow's strength.
Help me replace my worry with a simple trust in You.
Amen.

Why do you look down on another Christian? Remember, each of us will stand personally before the judgment seat of God.…So don't condemn each other anymore.
Romans 14:10,13

3

The First Tee

"It took me 17 years to get 3000 hits in baseball. I did it in one afternoon on the golf course."

—HANK AARON

The first tee is, without a doubt, one of the most glorious spots on God's green earth. The excitement is high, the anticipation invigorating. We select the right club. Flick grass skyward. Punch a tee into the ground. And hope no one is watching like they were the last time we missed the ball altogether.

The first tee can be a wonderful place, can't it? It can also be one of the most unnerving spots on the planet. Anticipation can give way to anxiety as we notice an impatient foursome behind us or a patio crammed with slightly inebriated golfers who carefully analyze our swing behind cupped hands, dissecting our stroke in whispers. For the most part, golfers are kind souls, but I have heard snickers, coughs, sputters, and the occasional muffled groan emanating from the patio after my first swing. I suppose the thing that's nice about being an imperfect golfer is the sheer delight it brings to others.

This makes me think of another place. A place that should be far more exhilarating than the first tee. And more forgiving, too. It is the church. How often we overlook our own shortcomings but notice the failures of other believers. I'm guilty of this. Perhaps you are too. Guilty of criticizing without a second thought and judging without a second chance. Sad, isn't it? The one place we should find the freedom to fail, we encounter judgment. The one place we should experience anticipation without anxiety feels a lot like the first tee at the country club.

Hockey Hall of Fame goalie Jacque Plante once joked, "How would you like a job where, if you made a mistake, a big red light came on and 18,000 people booed?" If you've ever been judged too harshly or gossiped about, you know how Jacque felt. Like a giant earthmover, some people move lots of dirt around—and they move it fast. Nothing makes a long story short like the arrival of the person being talked about. Proverbs has much to say about gossips. A gossip "betrays confidence" (11:13 NIV), "separates close friends" (16:28 NIV), and keeps a quarrel going (26:20). Gossip is straight from the pit. Don't participate in it. Don't receive it. Don't pass it on.

Those who easily judge forget that they, too, have stood on the first tee and duffed and struggled and hacked and made excuses. Understanding our own shortcomings helps us view the struggles of others with compassion and grace. When we judge others, we forget Jesus' frightening words in Matthew 7:2 (NIV): "For in the same way you judge others, you will be judged, and with the measure you use, it will be measured to you." Each of us stands before God deserving judgment, deserving shame. Instead we are offered grace. Let us extend it to others.

Have you been the victim of gossip lately? I have. Let us commit it to the Lord, who alone knows our hearts. And let us pray for the ones who have hurt us.

Are you judging people right now? I've been guilty of dissecting their "swing" from the patio. For this I need God's forgiveness and the wisdom to know that when I judge others, I condemn myself.

⚑

Dear Lord, forgive me for my judgmental spirit.
I so easily see the problems in others. Remind me of
my own imperfections, so that I may forgive them in others.
Thank You for Your amazing grace and forgiveness.
May I pass them along for Your sake. Amen.

May the God of hope fill you with all joy and
peace as you trust in him, so that you may overflow
with hope by the power of the Holy Spirit.
Romans 15:13 NIV

4

The Best Four-Letter Word

"I know I am getting better at golf because I
am hitting fewer spectators."

—GERALD FORD

Princess Anne of England is not a golfer. She once said, "Golf seems to me an arduous way to go for a walk. I prefer to take the dogs out." I understand completely. Sometimes golf irritates me, too. Sometimes it's like driving a unicycle through a car wash. Who needs this much punishment? But, even so, I keep going back to it, perhaps more than I should. The sign on my office door says it all:

This is the office of an avid golfer.
If it's a beautiful day,
chances are I called in sick.

I suppose my love for this sport has something to do with the fact that you can shoot the worst round of your life—you can hook, you can slice, you can hit the creek with a pocketful of balls—and still find yourself pulling another tee from the bag, punching it into the ground, cradling the ball atop it, and standing there like a fool thinking that maybe, just maybe, this one will go straight. Maybe today you'll break 90, or chip one into the cup, or putt from 30 feet out on a sloping green and watch the ball teeter on the edge…then drop.

We golfers live for that moment, don't we?

More than 500 golf courses opened last year in the United States alone, and I think the reason boils down to one four-letter word you don't hear often enough on the course. It is the one word that keeps us coming back.

> Each year more than 20 million people play on 13,000 courses in America.

Hope.

Golf is all about hope. The hope that on the next shot things will be different. That on the next shot something amazing will happen. That on the next shot things will change. We need hope on the golf course; we need it even more in life. Hope that things will improve, that this condition is not permanent, that something better lies ahead.

A friend called on a weekday morning. He's having trouble with his marriage. He asked me to golf with him, but what he really wanted to do was talk. And so we did. We talked about his life. About the mistakes behind him and the challenges ahead. Sometimes he pulled out a club, but mostly he talked. I golfed and listened. On the sixth hole we sat on the grass of the tee-off box, talking about golf and life. "The thing I love about golf," I told him, "is that each round is a fresh start. That's how it is with grace, too. In our lives, in our marriages, we won't get perfect

scores, but grace gives us another chance. Grace gives us
hope."

Hope for Christians is not found in our own goodness or ability, but in the unchanging promises offered us
by a risen Savior. In the darkest of times, hope can shine
the brightest. It emanates from the pages of Scripture. In
1 Peter we read, "Praise be to the God and Father of our
Lord Jesus Christ! In his great mercy he has given us
new birth into a living hope through the resurrection of
Jesus Christ from the dead, and into an inheritance…kept
in heaven for you" (1:3-4 NIV).

Hope opens doors that despair has slammed shut. Hope
looks for the good instead of harping on the worst. Hope
turns problems into opportunities and fear into faith.

Is such hope a pie-in-the-sky illusion? Does it make
Christians complacent, content to leave the world as it is?
Maybe so for some people, but knowing our future is
secure should free us to make a difference in the lives of
those around us.

Have you lost hope lately? If so, the writer of Hebrews
is speaking to you: "…Let us draw near to God with a
sincere heart in full assurance of faith, having our hearts
sprinkled to cleanse us from a guilty conscience and
having our bodies washed with pure water. Let us hold
unswervingly to the hope we profess, for he who promised
is faithful" (10:22-23 NIV).

Thank You, Lord, for the hope
You give through Your Son. Amen.

The tongue that brings healing is a tree of life.
Proverbs 15:4

5

My Son, Tiger

"Hit it hard. It will land somewhere."
—MARK CALCAVECCHIA

A revolutionary new golf club is about to be launched by a British firm. It promises to be the most powerful legal driver you can buy. At about $1,200 it should be. The club boasts a diamond face and the name DR4E (Diamonds Roll For Ever). "The reason it works is that diamonds are the hardest substance known to man," says Steven Knight, chairman of the company set to release it.

Will diamonds soon be a duffer's best friend? Will this club be the most powerful in existence as Steven claims? I don't know. But I do know of something even more powerful: the tongue. With tremendous potential for evil, it can also shape us for good.

Reminds me of a round of golf and a few choice words that changed my son forever. Last September I spoke at a golf tournament, so as always, I invited someone along.

That someone was Jeffrey, my grinning 12-year-old, blessed with an infectious laugh but little interest in the game of golf. Golf is boring, he thinks. It discourages him. The boy would rather eat cabbage ice cream.

"We'll throw in your brother's clubs," I told him, "but you don't have to golf. You can drive the cart and laugh at my shots." He seemed okay with that. After all, a trip with dad spells restaurants and hotels and waterslides to a boy his age. He can tolerate a game of golf for such rewards.

Upon arriving, we were introduced to the other members of our foursome, Jim and Neil, two of the kindest guys I've ever met. When they discovered Jeffrey's intentions, they were disappointed.

"Golf with us," pleaded Jim, bowing on one knee and extending a hand, "we need you."

"I'll buy you a pop and hamburger for lunch," promised Neil.

Perhaps it was the hamburger that beckoned louder than the golf course, but soon Jeffrey found himself on the first tee, addressing the ball and surprising us all with a straight shot about 100 yards down the fairway.

"Tiger!" said Jim. "You swing just like Tiger Woods!"

Jeffrey was grinning.

The tournament was a best ball format. From the first tee, my ball sailed 200 yards but found a bunker. Jim and Neil were less fortunate. So guess whose ball we used? You're right. It was "Tiger's."

Together the four of us managed to finish just under par that day, but "Tiger" doesn't remember the score. He remembers two middle-aged guys who were his biggest fans for 18 holes.

"That's okay," they'd say, when he duffed one. "Here, hit mine." And when the ball skimmed the grass, causing squirrels to scatter, they'd pat him on the back and say, "You're somethin', Tiger!"

Nearing home the next day, we passed the Three Hills Golf Club two miles west of town. "Dad," said Jeffrey, "let's go golfing." And a smile tugged at my face. Thanks to Jim and Neil, it was the first time in his life the boy had spoken those words.

The tongue can pack a wallop, can't it? A well-placed word can restore confidence, give purpose, and renew hope. It can uplift, nourish, and mend. Proverbs 16:24 says, "Kind words are like honey—sweet to the soul and healthy for the body." But our words also have the power to devastate. A few inconsiderate ones can cripple the spirit of a child, a spouse, or a friend. Proverbs 12:18 states that "reckless words pierce like a sword" (NIV).

If you're old like me, you may remember Karen Carpenter, part of the singing duo called "The Carpenters." They had more hits in the '70s than Pete Rose. Karen died unexpectedly of heart failure at age 32 after a longtime struggle with anorexia nervosa. *USA Today* reported that Karen's fatal obsession with weight control began when she read a reviewer's simple comment. He had dubbed her "Richard's chubby sister."

Yes, there is a time for speaking up and confronting. Such words when mixed with love can help us grow. But far more often our words need to be like those of my friends Jim and Neil—words that reflect God's love for us.

Every conversation is an opportunity. A chance to encourage or discourage, affirm the positive or dwell on the negative, celebrate victories or rehash failures, draw people to Christ or push them away. Neil and Jim may never know the impact they had on my son by being positive and uplifting. You may never know the eternal impact you make when you choose your words prayerfully and carefully.

One warning, though. If you live this way, people will want to golf with you. They will tell you their problems, share their joys, and open their hearts. You can even tell them about that new diamond driver. And follow up with something even more powerful, the tongue.

⛳

Help me understand the power of my words, Lord.
Help me say those things that will foster love,
peace, and growth in those I talk, golf, and live with.
Forgive me for words spoken in haste. Keep my tongue
from evil. May my words be like shampoo—rich,
concentrated, and seasoned with grace. Amen.

You need to persevere so that when you have done the will of
God, you will receive what he has promised.
Hebrews 10:36 NIV

6

Never Give Up

*"Ninety percent of putts that are short don't
go in."*

—YOGI BERRA

It was one of those days. I was one under. One under a bridge. One under a tree. One under the clubhouse. The only thing working in my bag was the bug spray. It seemed to be attracting them. My partner kept telling me to keep my head down—probably so I wouldn't see him laughing. I was using a new putter that day. My first one didn't float very well. I was hitting the woods just great...but I couldn't get out of them. I hit an eagle and a birdie. Also a deer and a coyote. I did break 90, though. And I was so excited I almost forgot to go on and play the second hole.

If you've played golf very long, chances are you've witnessed a fellow golfer walk off the course in disgust. Perhaps you've done so yourself. A friend of mine loves to tell the story (which he *claims* is true) of the preacher who was having a tough day and finally threw his clubs in the creek and stomped off. One of his three pals told the others, "He'll be back. You just watch. I give him five minutes." And sure enough, minutes later the preacher was back. Removing his shoes and socks and rolling up his pants, he waded into the creek. Fishing around for a moment, he pulled out the clubs. Then he unzipped a side pocket, pulled out his car keys, and hurled the clubs into even deeper water.

We smile because we've all been there. We've all felt like giving up. On the course. In life.

As I travel the country, parents tell me of wayward children who seem beyond the reach of prayer. People talk of marriages that seem beyond hope. A habit that seems unbreakable. A person who seems impossible.

> According to the National Hole-in-One Association, about 27 aces are scored per year after a golfer's ball hits a tree.

Four words tucked away in John 21:20 have been playing through my mind lately. The verse tells us that John "leaned back against Jesus" (NIV). Stop and read that again. I love those four words. We need to lean on Jesus, don't we? We need to stay on our knees and never give up.

> Therefore, since we are surrounded by such a great cloud of witnesses, let us throw off everything that hinders and the sin that so easily entangles, and let us run with perseverance the race marked out for us. Let us fix our eyes on Jesus, the author and perfecter of our faith, who for the joy set before him endured the cross, scorning its shame, and sat down at the right hand of the throne of God.

Consider him who endured such opposition
from sinful men, so that you will not grow
weary and lose heart (Hebrews 12:1-3 NIV).

The highest score ever recorded for *one* hole in a pro
tournament is a 23 by Tommy Armour on the seventeenth
hole in the 1927 Shawnee Open. But he stuck with it and
finished the round. This reminds me of Olympian Derek
Redmon.

In the 1992 Olympics, the British runner tore a liga-
ment midway through his race. As the rest of the runners
went on to finish, Derek lay on the ground, writhing in
pain. His hopes and dreams lay shattered on the track.

Then, as television cameras rolled, Derek pushed himself off the ground and began to run again, determined
to finish the race. But after a few short strides, his legs
buckled and he slowed to a walk. A man appeared on the
track then. Security guards tried to stop him, but he was
as determined as the runner. Putting his arm around
Derek's shoulder, he began coaxing him along. As the
crowd thundered its approval, the two crossed the finish
line. Together.

The man was Derek's father.

Your heavenly Father is cheering you on, too. So get
on your knees, lean on Jesus, and stay in the race.

⚐

*Lord, You know my heart. You know why I need to be
on my knees these days. Give me the strength
to persevere and the joy of seeing things through
to completion for Your glory. Amen.*

All athletes practice strict self-control. They do it to win a prize
that will fade away, but we do it for an eternal prize.
1 Corinthians 9:25

7

Crooked Golf

"Yes, even I am dishonest. Not in many ways,
but in some. Forty-one, I think it is."
—MARK TWAIN

I've learned some rather unsettling things about myself on the golf course. For one thing, I've discovered my propensity to cheat. I'm sorry if I shocked you there, but I must admit it. Once I slipped a replacement ball through a hole in the pocket of my pants. It was a devious trick a fellow golfer had used on me after he was unable to locate the ball he had shot. He ended up beating me by a stroke, and didn't repent until a year later. So the next time we played, I thought it was time for payback. I later apologized. Unfortunately, it wasn't the last time I needed to.

To this day, I must be careful, for the golf course can bring out the worst in me. An errant drive breeds frustration. A missed putt brings anger. And if it's a short putt, my fuse is even shorter. Few activities dissect a man better than golf. In my quest to win, to improve, to save face, I have stooped to amazing depths. Though I am seldom tempted to curse while grocery shopping, playing catch with my children, or sitting in church, take me to the golf course and the real Phil is lurking just beneath the serene surface, waiting to come out and play havoc. I'm ashamed to say that through the years the golf course has seen me curse quietly, yell loudly, and quit early.

The doctrine of original sin is much easier to grasp after I spend time on a golf course. The temptation to write down a wrong score or nudge a ball from a natural hazard helps me remember that I am a sinner. The prophet Jeremiah was possibly talking to golfers when he wrote: "The human heart is most deceitful and desperately wicked. Who really knows how bad it is?" (17:9).

There is incredible freedom in such an admission. In facing our own sinfulness, leaving it at the foot of the cross, and moving on, one stroke at a time. Each of us is a fragile creature whose hope does not lie in our own goodness, but in the fact that God sees that we are dust and loves us just the same.

Honesty is not just the first chapter in the book of wisdom; it is also the first chapter in the book of golf. If you've ever found yourself tallying scores with one whose memory is purposely poor, you know this. Charles Swindoll said these wise words: "Honesty has a beautiful and refreshing simplicity about it. No ulterior motives. No hidden meanings. An absence of hypocrisy, duplicity, political games, and verbal superficiality."

As honesty and integrity characterize our golf game and every area of our lives, there will be no need to put on a false front or live in fear of being caught.

When we face our sinfulness and repent of it, pretending is no longer in our bag of tricks. We have accepted the reality that we are sinners, that nothing we do will impress God. As a result, everything we do comes from thankfulness for all that He has done.

Now, it's time to sew up the pocket in those pants.

⚑

Lord, You know my heart. You know the times I've sinned against You today. Cleanse me. Forgive me. Change me. And do not reward me according to what I deserve, but in accordance with what Your amazing grace allows—a grace that is freely mine because of what Your only Son did on the cross. In Jesus' precious name, amen.

Do not be afraid, for I have ransomed you.
I have called you by name; you are mine.
Isaiah 43:1

8

The Card

*"Always keep in mind that if God didn't want
a man to have mulligans, golf balls wouldn't
come three to a sleeve."*

—DAN JENKINS

John was the resident pro at a local course seven years before he got up the nerve to try out for the PGA tour. With his new bride's encouragement, and the last of their savings, he flew to Florida, hoping to qualify at the PGA Qualifying School. After six rounds and 106 holes of playing his heart out, John was informed that he had finished among the top 35 golfers—good enough for his tour card. Before the tournament he had told himself he would wait until he got home to surprise his wife with the news. He struggled with his resolve while waiting in the airport barely able to resist the urge to dial her number. Finally he boarded the plane. After what seemed like an eternity, the flight landed, and an hour later John pulled into the driveway.

The house was quiet. In the kitchen he found a beautiful table set with their finest china. Lasagna, garlic toast, and a garden salad beckoned. Candles were lit. Could someone have tipped her off? Or did she just have that much faith in him?

His wife, Sara, strolled in from the living room, smiling, then listened excitedly to the good news. Wrapping her arms around him, she kissed him. Over dinner she listened to John's play-by-play description of those six rounds. Afterward, Sara pulled an envelope from the left pocket of her sweater. John ripped it open and pulled out a beautifully hand-lettered card. It read:

> Congratulations, Babe!
> I knew you could do it!
> I love you and I'm so proud of you.
> Yours forever, Sara

Needless to say, there was more kissing. Later, as the two were doing dishes together, a second envelope fell from Sara's other pocket. She tried to pick it up, but John beat her to it. Opening it, he read these words:

> I'm sorry, Honey.
> Please know that
> you'll always be a pro to me.
> I love you, and I'm proud of you
> no matter what.
> Yours forever, Sara

The story I made up; the message I did not. Receiving a tour card is nice, I'm sure. But can anything equal the gift of unconditional love? All of us long to be loved like that. Sprinkled throughout the diaries of atheist Madalyn Murray O'Hair was this simple phrase: "Somebody, somewhere, love me." If you have ever doubted the depths of God's love for you, listen to His words in Isaiah: "'Though the mountains be shaken and the hills be removed, yet my unfailing love for you will not be shaken…' says the LORD, who has compassion on you" (54:10 NIV).

There is a truth so simple that I almost hesitate to write about it. Yet I have met great preachers and missionaries and longtime saints for whom its absence has been devastating and its presence life-changing. It is the simple fact that there is nothing you can do to impress God. He already loves you. Before you were born, He died for you. He redeemed you. He called you by name. Second Timothy 1:9 says it so well: "It is God who saved us and chose us to live a holy life. He did this not because we deserved it, but because that was his plan long before the world began— to show his love and kindness to us through Christ Jesus."

No matter what has happened to you today, the handwritten card in God's pocket remains the same: "I am yours forever." No matter where you have strayed lately, His message has not changed: "Come home. I love you."

God can turn from His anger, but never from His love. Is there any better news in all the world?

ף

Thank You, Lord, for Your unconditional love. Thank You that I am valuable because You love me. May Your love within me overflow in everything I say and do. Amen.

*If one person falls, the other can reach out
and help. But people who are alone when they
fall are in real trouble.*
Ecclesiastes 4:10

9

The Perfect Foursome

*"Is my friend in the bunker, or is the jerk on
the green?"*
—JAMES ENNS

When I was a boy my father told me to treat my
friends as I would my golf clubs. "Take them out often,
son," he said, "and never let them beat you." Unfortunately
friends do beat me from time to time—some more often
than others—but I've discovered that golf is the perfect
team sport. It's best enjoyed with a few good friends.

The first member of my ideal foursome is Vance Neudorf who, by his own admission, is a hacker-golfer. He tells
jokes while I putt. "So," he whispers, as I draw the putter
back in a smooth pendulum motion, "do your clubs have
numbers on them? Mine don't."

I once threatened to beat the stuffing out of him right
there on the green, but I've settled for laughing and
mailing him the scorecard after each round. Vance is one
of my best friends, but he golfs only when there are no

other options. Vance stands too close to the ball—after he hits it. He insists that golf is cow-pasture pool and a poor excuse for a sport. The only way you can get hurt playing golf, he believes, is to get struck by lightning. One day I watched him lose every ball in his bag on the seventh hole. He changed his tune that day. Sometimes golf *can* hurt you. "Golf," he muttered through his teeth, "is an expensive way of playing marbles." Sometimes Vance is so bad that he considers renting a bucket of balls just to practice his drop.

Gord Robideau is an avid golfer in the sense that if he had to choose between playing a round and ensuring world peace, he would want to know how many holes. Gord is a schoolteacher. For him, golf is science, art, and physics all rolled into one class. When we play together, the competition is high. On the first hole, Gord stretches at length before teeing off. Then he tosses tufts of grass in the air, holds a wet finger to the wind, and talks to the ball: "All right, little buddy," he says, "let's you and me be friends all day. I'll swing…you say wonderful." When Gord and I play, the score is often tied, or one beats the other by a stroke.

The worst loss in a playoff? Al Espinosa finished 23 strokes behind Bobby Jones in the 1929 U.S. Open.

Jeff Crouch is a golfer with very few handicaps. He earns a living teaching golf to Minnesotans when their weather is good (July 4–18). When we play, I spend the time apologizing for my banana slice and trying to think of synonyms for "marvelous." (I apologize to readers in Minnesota. Next time I will pick on Iowa.)

In thinking about these friends, it strikes me that ideally each of us needs three kinds of friends to help us along the course of life. A friend we can hang out with, one we can hang onto, and one we can help. The foursome is not a biblical number, but it is a practical one. Two can lie about their scores easier than four. Two can lead each other astray, while four can guard against this.

David and Jonathan hung out together. They played with slingshots and arrows and very likely enjoyed some form of golf involving shepherds' staffs and snake holes and sand traps in the desert. First Samuel 18:1 NIV tells us that Jonathan loved David "as he loved himself." What a tribute! Jesus was criticized for being a friend of sinners (see Matthew 11:19 NIV). That's quite an indictment, isn't it? Could the same be said of me? Abraham was called "the friend of God" (James 2:23). Wouldn't you like that on your tombstone? I would. Ultimately God is the friend who will stick with us when others walk out. He is one we can hang onto. And He will bring friends into our lives to help us through the tough times.

A good friend is like an accurate putter—hard to find. What kind of friend are you?

⚑

Lord, help me to be there when others need me.
May I be accused one day of being a friend of sinners and,
most of all, being a friend of God. Amen.

Make me walk along the path of your commands,
for that is where my happiness is found.
Psalm 119:35

10

Rules of Enjoyment

"Golf…makes liars out of honest men, cheats
out of altruists, cowards out of brave men, and
fools out of everybody."

—MILTON GROSS

One of my favorite golf stories from a PGA event involves a guy named Ben. Born January 11, 1952, Ben grew up watching from the golf cart as his father Charlie played. While other fathers pushed or coaxed their sons into it, Ben's father didn't need to. The boy couldn't help noticing how much his dad loved the game. At the age of six, Ben played his first round. In fourth grade, he won his first tournament, the Casis Elementary Open, with a score of 96. Continuing to improve, he shot a 74 for 18 holes when he was only 10. "When I finally got to play regularly," he would later tell a reporter, "all my dad said was I'd have to learn how to play the right way and by the rules."

Nineteen PGA victories and $7 million later, Ben Crenshaw is still playing by the rules. He's also finding out that sometimes those rules hurt. During one tournament, Crenshaw's ball found the top of a palm tree. His

dedicated caddie climbed a ladder and shook the tree vig-
orously. A ball fell down and bounced in the rough. They
examined it. It wasn't Crenshaw's. So the caddie shook the
tree some more. Another fell. And another. In all, the
caddie shook two dozen golf balls from the tree that day.
Not one of them belonged to Crenshaw. The Texas native
was forced to take a penalty.

Have the rules of golf ever gotten in
the way of your score? Some of them are
downright intriguing. For instance, did
you know that if your ball is in the fairway
resting against a twig and you pull the twig
away causing the ball to move, it will cost
you a stroke? It's true. But if the ball rests
against a candy wrapper and the same
thing happens, there's no penalty. The
wrapper is not considered a natural object.

> Local rule at Jinga Golf Course in Uganda: If a ball comes to rest in dangerous proximity to a crocodile, another ball may be dropped.

Let's say your ball lands in a bunker
and is covered by leaves (happens to me
all the time). You remove enough leaves
with your club to enable you to see part
of the ball. No problem. But as you address the ball, you
touch some of the leaves with your club. If golf had a referee, he'd blow the whistle on you.

Golf started out a simple game. Then the Scots got
hold of it and started printing rule books. The bigger the
books, the more they could charge. (I'm kidding, Dad!)
Today, a game played with 14 clubs and a dozen balls has
thousands of rules—and more are added each year. Sometimes those rules irritate me. They seem unfair. Strict.
Inhibiting. Though I'm sure they were created so I might
enjoy the game, sometimes I wonder.

Perhaps you've felt the same about the rules God has established. They seem unfair. Stifling. Rigid. A list of divine Dos and Don'ts. But is it possible that those laws were established for our benefit, our protection, and, yes, ultimately for our pleasure?

When pro golfer Seve Ballesteros was asked whether or not he was monogamous, the Spaniard responded, "That would be like playing the same golf course all the time." I don't know if Seve was joking, but I do know that he was dead wrong. The lasting joy God gives when we follow the laws He has designed for us far outweigh the temporary pleasures sin offers.

It's not easy explaining to a two-year-old why eating four pounds of Swiss chocolate may be a bad idea. But as you hold his head over the sink an hour later, he understands. If you've stood by "the sink" with others who have been broken by the consequences of their own sin, you understand. What we sacrifice for momentary pleasure is astronomical. What God requires of us is for our best. Our Creator knows and loves us. As surely as the planets and stars function best within His laws, so will we.

Ben Crenshaw once said that the reward from obeying the rules of golf "has been the incredible enjoyment I've gotten from the game."

So it can be with us. The surest pathway to pleasure comes through obedience, in service to others and to our God.

🏴

*Lord, thank You for the rules of life laid down
that I might experience Your pleasure. Thank You that
though Your laws show me how crooked I am, Your Son
straightened me out—with grace. May I operate not from
obligation, but from love for You and others. Amen.*

So take a new grip with your tired hands and stand firm on your shaky legs. Mark out a straight path for your feet. Then those who follow you, though they are weak and lame, will not stumble and fall but will become strong.
Hebrews 12:12-13

11

My Hall of Fame

"If this was the ultimate game, they wouldn't be playing it again next year."
—DWAYNE THOMAS, OF THE DALLAS COWBOYS,
WHEN ASKED ABOUT SUPERBOWL WEEK

Did you read today's verse? If not, go ahead. I'll wait. Sounds like the verse was written for us golfers, don't you think? A new grip. Tired hands. Shaky legs. A straight path for our feet.

While you think of that verse, let me ask you something else. Can you name the top ten golfers in the world? Give it a try. Can you name the last five to wear a green jacket at the Masters? How about the winners of the Ryder Cup, the World Series, or the Stanley Cup? If you can, you are truly amazing (you have also spent way too much time with the remote control). But chances are you couldn't. Chances are you're like me. Such forgetfulness is a gentle reminder that today's sports headlines fade into tomorrow. Standing ovations end. Applause dies down. Awards collect dust. Things we thought so important today are forgotten next week. "Failure," perhaps, could be defined as succeeding at something that doesn't really matter.

Recently, at a team chapel, I spoke with a major league ball team. I talked about true success. The men listened carefully, and, for a few of them, the tears started to come. These were men who had reached the pinnacle of success, but their questions about life were the same as mine. What is true success? How do I have an eternal impact? One particular question lit up their faces. "Can you remember," I asked, "one person who encouraged you when you were young?"

How would you respond? Could you name a friend who sat beside you during a tough time? A youth worker who cared when no one else seemed to? A pastor who said something you badly needed to hear? An older person who encouraged you?

It's a little easier than naming the last three Superbowl champs, I hope.

I suppose the people we remember are not the ones with the most credentials or the most cash. They are the ones who loved us enough to care. They stood firm, as our verse says, and gave us an example to follow.

I can't name two of the wealthiest people on earth, but I can tell you stories of those who have enriched my life beyond measure. Golf has its Hall of Fame. So does hockey. And Hollywood. And Nashville. But if I were constructing Phil's Hall of Fame, I think I'd start with some unknown and relatively unlettered people who were somehow able to look past my faults and see what God could do.

My praying parents would be first. And the exhibit would include people like Mr. Al Bienert. You see, I would

likely not be writing this book without the impact of this
godly man who took me aside in high school. I was fright-
ened at first. He was the teacher; I was the student. I
hadn't done a thing right since kindergarten, it seemed,
and teachers did not appreciate me. But Mr. Bienert saw
something different. "I think you have a gift in the area
of communication. I'd like you in my Communications
Arts class," he said, thereby becoming the first teacher in
world history to want me in his class.

Next up would be Vera Nicolson. This gentle Aus-
tralian is 92 years young, and she prays for me every day.
It's not just because I need it; it's because she believes God
wants her to. She's the kind who reads a Bible verse, then
does what it says. She hasn't golfed a round in her life, but
I thank God for the straight path she has shown me by
her example.

A dozen more people come to mind. Each is a
reminder that success in life has nothing to do with low-
ering my score, though that would be nice. Success in life
has nothing to do with money, though there are times
we'd all like a little more. Success has to do with the direction we point out to the ones who follow us.

Who would you put in your hall of fame? What can
you learn from them today?

*Thank You, dear Lord, for those who have had an eternal
impact on me. Help me follow in their footsteps. Amen.*

And this is what he requires: to do what is right,
to love mercy, and to walk humbly with your God.
Micah 6:8

12

Improving Your Lie

*"Golf is the infallible test....The man who can
go into a patch of rough alone, with the
knowledge that only God is watching him, and
play his ball where it lies is the man who will
serve you faithfully and well."*

— P.G. WODEHOUSE

If you want to find out what a friend is truly like, play golf with him or her. Perhaps there is no other place where our true character so easily bubbles to the surface.

For instance, my friend Gord is a died-in-the-wool cheater. Nothing increases his score like witnesses. One day, while we were golfing together, he claimed to have found his ball in the rough. I knew he was lying, the big cheat. I had already picked up his ball and placed it in my pocket.

No other game depends on the integrity of the individual player so much as golf. There is no referee, no line judge, no instant replay camera. Hockey players are not asked to skate to the penalty box voluntarily, nor do football players raise their hands when they jump offside. But this is what golf requires: absolute integrity.

How is your Integrity Quotient? Grab a pencil and find out!

The Golfer's Integrity Quiz

1. Have you ever improved your lie when you thought no one was looking? ❑ Yes ❑ No

2. Have you taken a Mulligan without another's consent? ❑ Yes ❑ No

3. Have you ever kicked your ball from behind a tree while pointing to some wildlife? ❑ Yes ❑ No

4. Did you ever deliberately miss a short putt to drive up your handicap? ❑ Yes ❑ No

5. Have you "inched" a putt by placing your marker in front of the ball, then your ball in front of the marker? ❑ Yes ❑ No

6. Did you ever miss the ball completely on the downswing and not count the stroke? ❑ Yes ❑ No

7. Have you ever given yourself a gimme?
❑ Yes ❑ No

8. Have you ever made fun of someone who takes rules like these seriously? ❑ Yes ❑ No

9. Do you agree with Mark Twain that "fewer things are harder to put up with than the annoyance of a good example"? ❑ Yes ❑ No

If you answered "yes" to any of these questions, you are a cheater. If you answered "no" to all of these questions, you are a liar. If your answers were mixed, well, you are both. (I hope you are smiling at this point.)

It's interesting that this sport, which requires absolute integrity, has become so popular in a society that has, for the most part, discarded absolutes. In *The Day America Told the Truth*, James Patterson and Peter Kim estimate that 91 percent of us regularly lie. The examples are endless. Tim Johnson, former manager of the Toronto Blue Jays invented a Vietnam War record for himself. Football coach George O'Leary was caught fabricating details for his resume (it cost him his dream job as coach of Notre Dame). Jerry Reinsdorf, coowner of the Chicago Whitesox, once said, "I know when George Steinbrenner is lying. His lips move."

Recently, here in Canada, more than 40 college students in the same class submitted the same paper, downloaded from the Internet. These students were not the sharpest tools in the shed. When asked about it, one of them said, "We've been under a lot of stress lately." "Throw out the rulebook," such a person might reason. "If a lie does more help than harm, feel free to employ one."

> In sixteenth-century Scotland, Sunday golfers were fined 40 shillings for skipping church to play.

The ultimate Rulebook instructs us otherwise. In Psalm 15, David asked, "Who may worship in your sanctuary, LORD?...Those who lead blameless lives and do what is right, speaking the truth from sincere hearts.... [those who] keep their promises even when it hurts" (verses 1-2,4).

From an early age, Tom had his heart set on becoming a champion. In the first state tournament he entered, he put his putter down behind the ball on one of the greens. The ball moved slightly, but no one saw it—except for

Tom. He wanted to win in the worst way, but he knew what was best. "My ball moved," he told an official, placing his personal integrity above his desire to win. The action cost him the hole. But Tom Watson went on to win the match, a host of championships, and the respect and admiration of people the world over.

Integrity may cost you a hole or two. It may even cost you the game. But it also will earn you the peace of an unblemished conscience and the joy of hearing your Savior say, "Well done, my good and faithful servant."

May your trophy case be adorned with the lasting honor of integrity.

Now, I better write a letter of apology to my friend Gord.

⚑

Lord, may I walk before You with a blameless heart. Amen.

I am going to prepare a place for you....I will come and get you, so that you will always be where I am.
John 14:2-3

13

Heavenly Golf

"If there's no golf in heaven, then I'm not going!"
—POPULAR SIGN

For centuries, theologians have debated topics such as predestination, existentialism, ecclesiology, and other words I can't spell. When they get home after a long day of doing this, their children ask them more practical questions like, "How can I get ink out of your Sunday shirt, Daddy?" or "Why doesn't glue stick to the inside of the bottle?"

Questions. We all have them, don't we?

I was golfing with a pastor one day, and the subject shifted to heaven. "So," he asked somewhat reluctantly, "do you think there will be golf in heaven?" I was lining up an 8-foot putt at the time, and the question did little to aid my concentration. After three-putting, I told him the joke about the angel who suddenly appeared to a man who was golfing at Pebble Beach. The angel said, "I can answer any question you want, so go ahead and ask." The man thought for a moment. "Are there golf courses in heaven?" The angel replied, "Do you want the good news or the bad news first?" The man shrugged. "The good news." So the angel told him, "The courses in heaven are so beautiful I can scarcely describe them. There are no green fees, you have your choice of clubs, and electric carts are provided free of charge. All the balls miraculously jump from the rough and float on water so you'll never lose them, and the cups are six inches in diameter."

The golfer smiled and asked, "What's the bad news?"

"Well," the angel said, "I booked you for a tee time in five minutes."

The pastor laughed a little louder than I anticipated, then backed away from his ball and made a startling and honest admission: "You know, I don't really want to go to heaven...all that worship...it seems boring to me." For one of the few times in my life, I was speechless.

We earthlings cling to this life. We try desperately to preserve and prolong it. We spend billions of dollars each year trying to look younger, trying to stall chronic baldness, and trying to halt the inevitable onslaught of old age. When I was 21, I didn't want Jesus to come back until I was married. (There were a few times after marriage that I prayed He would!) My daughter once told me that if our dog wasn't going to heaven, she didn't want to go there, either. I understand the feeling.

In 1973, Arthur Thompson shot a round of 103 in British Columbia. He was 103.

But think about it. Would we really choose a place that reeks of suffering and death, of bankruptcies and divorce, of school shootings and brutal wars over the paradise God is preparing? If so, Satan has truly blinded us to the realities of heaven.

The apostle Paul said that to depart and be with Christ was "far better" than staying on earth (Philippians 1:23). Ecclesiastes 3:11 tells us that God "has planted eternity in the human heart." We have within us hopes, needs, and longings that the very best marriage, the best worship time, and the best golf course cannot completely fulfill. Only Jesus Christ can truly satisfy our thirst. As C.S. Lewis wrote, "If I find in myself a desire which no experience in this world can satisfy, the most probable explanation is that I was made for another world."

I wonder how God feels when He sees us hanging on so tightly to this gopher-infested golf course with sand greens like the ones I played on as a kid, dreading the home He has been creating. It's a little like trying to explain the pleasures of driving a Ferrari to a two-year-old who would rather play with a cardboard box.

Life in this world is really just the preparation—the driving range, if you will. What comes at the end is the beginning of the greatest round imaginable, where every hole is more exciting than the one before. And so I would not trade a thousand rounds at Pebble Beach with Tiger Woods, Arnold Palmer, and David Duval for one moment with the Savior.

Is there golf in heaven? I don't know. Like you, I hope so. And I hope there's hockey, too. (I'll have my teeth back!) And chocolate. And colors we haven't yet seen. But I do know this: it won't be on our mind when we arrive. You see, the one who loves us most and knows our every longing will be there with His hands outstretched

to welcome us home. And life with Him will be out of
this world.

꒛

Thank You, Father, for the hope of heaven.
Thank You for making it possible for me to enter
through the death of Your Son.
May my longing for home make me more effective here.
Amen.

Live according to your new life in the Holy Spirit.
Then you won't be doing what your sinful nature craves.
Galatians 5:16

14

The Old Slice

*"I don't care to join any club that's prepared
to have me as a member."*
—GROUCHO MARX

For me, the easiest shot in all of golf is my fourth putt. On the same green. Next to that, I am probably most comfortable chipping. As a teenager, I spent hours in the backyard with my wedge, aiming balls by the buckets at tiny objects. By the time I was finished, so was the yard (just ask my mother). But the exercise paid rich dividends. In 30 years of golfing, I have a number of eagles to my credit—all courtesy of a short club with PW on the bottom.

There are other clubs in my bag, however. Clubs that have caused me grief since day one. At the top of the list is the longest club I own: my 1-wood.

Put me on the tee box of any par five, and I get the shakes. You see, I usually hit a straight ball, but place a driver in my hands, and I'll show you a slice you can set your watch by. For me, driving straight is the most difficult maneuver in the sports world, with the possible exception of going to a baseball game and buying hot dogs for my children without getting mustard on my pants.

On a recent trip to beautiful British Columbia, I had an hour to spare, so I found a golf course, put some funny-shaped coins in a ball machine, and lugged two sizeable buckets to the driving range. After chipping awhile, I wandered over to the Pro Shop and asked if I could test drive a Callaway wood. The pro was happy to take my Visa card, then he duct-taped the head so I wouldn't damage the $500 club. Stepping up to the rubber tee, I began slicing one ball after another toward the right field fence. The pro was watching my every hit.

"Must be the club," I said, grinning at him.

He smiled.

"Do you have a minute?" I asked.

He kindly walked over and stood behind me.

"Can you tell what I'm doing wrong?"

"It's your elbow," he said immediately. "It's stuck to your rib cage. Try again. Let the elbow go. Bring your hands straight through."

Sam Snead holds the record for appearing in the most Masters. His first set of clubs, purchased in the 1920s, cost him $9.50.

I tried it. And wouldn't you know it. For the first time in three years, I hit one straight as an arrow—almost knocking over the 250-yard marker.

"It's a miracle!" I said. "How much do I owe you?" He laughed. "I'll just keep your Visa card."

When he returned to the Pro Shop, however, I returned to my old habits. After all, that slice took me 30 years to develop. I wasn't about to give it up that easily. And three days later my elbow was still glued to my ribs. I was hitting 40 yards to the right of the target every time. It's frustrating, embarrassing, painful. And the worst part is knowing that the same thing happens in my walk with God. It happened to the apostle Paul, too. Listen to his words:

> No matter which way I turn, I can't make myself do right. I want to, but I can't. When I want to do good, I don't. And when I try not to do wrong, I do it anyway....I love God's law with all my heart. But there is another law at work within me that is at war with my mind. This law wins the fight and makes me a slave to the sin that is still within me. Oh, what a miserable person I am! (Romans 7:18-19,22-24).

Sound familiar? Any growing and transparent believer will admit to an inner battle with recurring habits, temptations, and sins. How good to know that we are not alone. How much better to know that there is a solution! "Who will free me from this life that is dominated by sin?" asks Paul. "Thank God! The answer is in Jesus Christ our Lord" (Romans 7:24-25).

With daily direction from the Master, we can walk victoriously. Notice that I didn't say without sin. But God will increase our hatred of sin as we draw near to Him, walking in His power, by His Holy Spirit.

Consider these liberating words from Romans 8:1: "So now there is no condemnation for those who belong to Christ Jesus. For the power of the life-giving Spirit has freed you through Christ Jesus from the power of sin that leads to death."

I hope to remember those words the next time I find my elbow glued to my rib cage.

⚑

Lord, give me a sensitivity to Your Spirit, a deep hatred of sin in my life, and an increased love for righteousness.
Amen.

*We do not make requests of you because
we are righteous, but because of your great mercy.*
Daniel 9:18 NIV

15

Mulligans

*"The term 'mulligan' is really a contraction of
the phrase 'maul it again.'"* *"Mulligan: invented
by an Irishman who wanted to hit one more
twenty-yard grounder."*

—JIM BISHOP

In football you get four downs. In baseball, three
strikes. In tennis you get two serves, and in basketball
you get a rebound. But not in golf. In golf, one shot is all
you have. The next shot. And, unlike baseball, golf requires
that you play your foul balls...unless you count mulligans.

The mulligan, in case you didn't have time to study it
in college, was invented by one of my fellow Canadians
back in the late 1920s. According to myth, legend, and
obscure golf history books, David Mulligan and a group
of friends enjoyed frequent rounds at St. Lambert Country
Club, outside Montreal, Quebec. Because David had the
only automobile, he was the designated driver. (I'm sure
his kind Canadian companions helped him with the gas.)

The trip traversed rough roads, most of them dirt and gravel. An especially bumpy bridge guarded the entrance to the course. Because Mulligan's hands suffered the shock of the vibrating steering wheel, his friends graciously awarded him a second shot off the first tee. Ever since, golfers have been inventing their own excuses for awarding themselves a mulligan. These include: "The pros warm up on the driving range before they drive"; "You were talking"; "I was talking"; "I'm quite sure a plane flew over"; and "I came here in a Chevy."

Though the mulligan is taboo on the pro tour, most friendly matches employ some form of it. You can "buy" a mulligan at many tournaments for five dollars. Some computer golf games afford you unlimited mulligans. A friend of mine refers to the shot as a "do-over."

Unfortunately, the golf course is one of a very few places that allows us ordinary folk mulligans. In the film *City Slickers*, a threesome of best buddies sets off on a two-week cattle drive, hoping to leave behind a multitude of midlife crises. One of the characters, played by Daniel Stern, confesses to the others that he has had an affair and ruined his marriage. They remind him of a game they played as kids. A game that included a "do-over."

But in real life we don't get do-overs—or mulligans. Sin pays deadly dividends. The hurt we've caused may linger for decades. Words said in an instant can bring heartache for years. Trust built over a lifetime can be destroyed in seconds. At times, we long to turn the clock back. We long for a friend, a spouse, or a child to say, "No problem, do it again." Some of us even find God's forgiveness too much to hope for.

When I was younger, I thought of Him as the big scorekeeper in the sky. Every time I stepped out of line, He gave me another stroke. Every lie brought another tick mark; every lustful thought or angry outburst called for a severe penalty.

And then I discovered God's mercy.

The author of the world's most well-loved hymn experienced that mercy. As first mate on an English slave ship, John Newton was plunged into a world of violence, rape, and merciless oppression. At that time, Newton's rejection of God wasn't enough. He also made it a point to mock and destroy the faith of any believing crewman. At one point, his own wicked behavior landed him in chains, where he found himself at the mercy of the very slaves he was selling. They could have beaten him or cursed him. Instead, they took pity on him.

While sailing back to England, a terrible storm took the life of one of the sailors, and the question began to haunt Newton: If you die tonight, where will you spend eternity? Remembering those slaves and the words "Christ died for sinners," Newton fell to his knees and begged forgiveness.

"I see no reason why the Lord singled me out for mercy," he later wrote, "unless it was to show, by one astonishing instance, that with Him nothing is impossible."

Today, Newton's hymns are sung around the world, and at the top of the hit list is his most famous: "Amazing Grace."

> Amazing grace, how sweet the sound, that saved a wretch like me. I once was lost but now am found, was blind but now I see...

His epitaph reads, "John Newton...once an infidel and libertine, a servant of slaves in Africa, was, by the rich mercy of our Lord and Savior, Jesus Christ, preserved, pardoned, and appointed to preach the faith he had long labored to destroy."

"Praise be to the God and Father of our Lord Jesus Christ! In his great mercy he has given us new birth into a living hope through the resurrection of Jesus Christ from the dead" (1 Peter 1:3 NIV).

Thank God for the divine "mulligan" called mercy.

⚑

I praise You, Lord, for Your mercy. Thank You
for offering me the ultimate do-over. May I pass along
some mulligans today, offering others this gospel of grace.
Amen.

*For I am not ashamed of this Good News
about Christ. It is the power of God at work,
saving everyone who believes.*
Romans 1:16

16

Risky Business

*"Golf is good for the soul. You get so mad at
yourself you forget to hate your enemies."*
—WILL ROGERS

Have you ever made a fool of yourself on the golf course? Believe me, I have. I once hit nothing but air with my 3-wood (only to have the ball fall off the tee, defy physics, and roll backward). I've watched a 7-iron fly from my hands, only to land in a muddy creek (yes, I went in after it). I've found that the shortest distance between any two points on the golf course is a direct line that passes through the woods. One time in Quebec, I rattled an errant 5-iron shot around a metal clubhouse roof while two complete strangers said things I did not understand, in a language I did not speak.

Golf is risky busines. When we venture onto the golf course, we risk failure. We risk being laughed at, ridiculed, or made to look silly. We risk having golfers turn the other way when we swing. They may stifle a laugh. Or disguise it in a cough. As with anything worthwhile in life, golf demands a certain unguardedness, a willingness to take risks—including the risk of making a fool of oneself or, at the very least, being thought of as one. In many ways, it would be easier to stay at home.

This reminds me of the risks we take when we share our faith. I've failed so often at it that sometimes I wish I'd stayed at home. But I'm beginning to discover that I don't need the wisdom of a rocket scientist or the pulpit of Billy Graham. I need only to be myself.

One afternoon I golfed with a gentleman who pulled a large bottle of vodka from his bag after his very first drive (if you saw his drive, you'd understand why).

"You want some?" he asked.

I told him my slice was bad enough without it.

"What's your name?" he said, introducing himself.

"Phil Callaway," I told him.

"Do you make the clubs?" he asked.

"No," I replied, "I pay people to do that." Of course, I quickly told him the truth. And it was a good thing. When the conversation got past golf and the weather, it didn't take him long to discover that I was a Christian.

"I've had awful experiences with Christians," he blurted.

"Really?" I said rather excitedly, "Me, too."

My response opened the door for a lengthy discussion—and, for some reason, closed the lid on the vodka bottle. As we walked the course together, I noticed something else. I noticed how my new friend watched me. He watched my response to hitting a bunker. Or hitting the creek. Or missing a putt. And as we said goodbye later that afternoon, he thanked me. "I've got some things to think about," he said.

Colossians 4:5 advises us to "live wisely among those who are not Christians, and make the most of every opportunity." That does not mean pinning Romans 3:23 ("for all have sinned…") to our shirts before each match, dropping Gospels of John on the fairway, or even having every answer. It simply means seizing each chance we are given to live out our faith. Our job is not to save the world—God already did that. But we should use every opportunity to help people realize it.

> In 1962, meteorologist Nils Lied hit a golf ball 2,640 yards across ice in Antarctica.

What do others see when they watch you golf? Whether we'd like them to or not, people are watching the way we live our lives. And nothing seems to show them their need for Christ more effectively than seeing the way He helps us respond to the sand traps of life. A Monday-night men's league may be the best pulpit you'll have all week!

Lord, may others see You in me.
Help me to realize that sharing my faith
is not a part-time occupation,
but a way of life.
Amen.

Teach us to make the most of our time,
so that we may grow in wisdom.
Moses, Psalm 90:12

17

One Golfer's Legacy

"It is since Christians have largely ceased to think of the other world that they have become so ineffective in this [one].

—C.S. LEWIS

Unless you've been living on one of Saturn's rings for the last decade or two, chances are you've heard of Tiger Woods. But the odds are equally as good that you have not heard of Lewis Chitengwa, the budding Zimbabwe superstar who was good enough to chase Tiger away from the trophy at the Orange Bowl International Junior Championship in 1992. The next year Lewis made headlines, becoming the first black man to win the South African men's amateur championship in 1993—a feat often referred to as the golfing equivalent of Jackie Robinson's achievement in baseball.

As I was writing this book, Lewis, who gave up a promising soccer career to pursue golf, was playing at the Edmonton Open, less than three hours from my front door. On Saturday, he became ill and was admitted to the hospital with flulike symptoms. Hours later, the 26-year-old was pronounced dead at the University of Alberta hospital, a victim of meningococcemia, a deadly strain of meningitis. PGA star Nick Price, a personal friend and business partner, was "devastated by the news," as were the other golfers who played the final round. The usual fist-pumping after long putts found the bottom of cups was noticeably missing. The customary thrashing and whacking of clubs after errant shots had disappeared.

Few things—not even the $150,000 up for grabs—seemed to matter.

Fittingly, the final round began with gray clouds and warm rain falling from the heavens. At the top of every leaderboard was the message, "God speed, Lewis."

"You'd see that, you'd see where you stood and say, 'Who cares?'" said Aaron Barber, who shot a 65 and claimed a two-stroke victory that day. "Lewis put things in perspective. We're just playing a game for a living, and it is nothing more than that. Death touches everyone, especially our friends. I could have shot a 90 today. It was of no consequence. Usually playing in the final group on the last day I would be more nervous. I wasn't at all. It just didn't matter. The edge was taken off golf today."

> The longest recorded putt in a major? Nick Faldo's 100-foot birdie in the 1989 Masters.

The trophy has been renamed in his honor now. A Lewis Chitengwa Memorial Tournament will be held in Charlottesville, Virginia, and a scholarship will be established to benefit his two brothers and two sisters back home. But of even greater significance is the legacy he left behind for friends, family, and fellow golfers.

"From wherever he was in the world, Lewis would always phone on my 10-year-old son's birthday," said one friend.

"He was caring, generous, thoughtful," said a rival golfer. Others described him as kind, respectful, and blessed with a good sense of humor.

The subdued atmosphere among the players had much to do with Lewis' death, but perhaps even more to do with the way he lived his life. "He was one in a million," said a close friend, "You only meet a few people in your life like him. He was a very devout Christian with all the right values."

There's nothing quite like death to remind us of what really matters. Some people impact us by what they do, but more often by who they are.

Lewis Chitengwa admired his hero, Nick Price, and he loved golf instructional books. But his life was patterned after another hero, Jesus Christ.

And those who cleared his personal effects from the room he had been staying in that week discovered the true guidebook he turned to in life. Chitengwa's Bible was open beside his bed.

Thank You, Lord, for those who have impacted me
with their faith, their thoughtfulness, or simple phone calls.
I may never stand before a gallery of admiring fans,
but help me spend the short time You have given me on earth
to leave the right legacy. For Your glory, amen.

A cheerful heart is good medicine,
but a broken spirit saps a person's strength.
Proverbs 17:22

18

Laughing Matters

"I may be the only golfer never to have broken
a single putter, if you don't count the one I
twisted into a loop and threw into a bush."
—Thomas Boswell

I played a joke on a friend this summer. At least I think he's still my friend. "You shoot first," I told him on the first tee. "I'll shoot second. My swing is so amazing right now that if you can reach my ball with a pitching wedge on your second shot, you can choose six balls from my bag."

He thought about it, then grinned. And laughed. And swung away. His ball bounced to a stop about 200 yards down the left side of the fairway.

"Beat that," he chuckled, walking over to my bag and unzipping a pouch on the side. I didn't say anything. Just stepped up to the tee and took a practice swing. Then I turned 180 degrees and drove my ball over a creek and into a cow pasture 400 yards from his. I think my friend is still laughing.

I hope you'll agree that it's okay to have fun on the golf course. I, for one, play better when I'm in a good humor. I love to lower my handicap, but a round of golf in which I do not laugh is a losing round, no matter what my score. Some people disagree. In Walkersville, Maryland, a golfer filed a $500,000 lawsuit against a friend and the friend's country club after he was handed a mustard-covered mouse as a practical joke. Some friend. Good thing they didn't put a skunk in his bag.

Golf is serious stuff for some people. For them, every hole is the eighteenth at the Masters. They've got yardage binoculars in one pocket and a pencil sharpener in the other. Their idea of a good time is memorizing the rulebook in Latin.

You'll find such people in church, too. The Christian life leaves no room for laughter, they believe. I get letters from them often. One wrote, "What does laughing have to do with being a Christian? You need to get serious." I wrote him a kind letter. Then I went to his home and stuffed an apple in his exhaust pipe (okay, not really).

Laughter is not always easy to come by. Life is difficult. Times are tough. Yet I am convinced that few things are more important in an age such as ours than a good sense of humor. It's impossible to laugh and worry at the same time. Stress and fear are incompatible with a good guffaw. Laughter is tax-free, has no MSG, no fat grams that we know of, and, if you mix it with some hope, it won't shrink as you grow older.

Pro golfers Greg Norman and Craig Wood have lost all four Majors in playoffs.

Scientists tell us that 20 seconds of laughter produces the same effect on the body as 3 minutes of strenuous rowing. I don't know if that's true, but laughter has never started a war, ended a relationship, or committed a crime. It's one of the few things that costs us nothing these days.

Laughter got me in trouble only twice in my life: once in the back row of a church during a sermon and once when my wife was expecting and asked me, "Honey, do I look fat?" I want you to know that I have learned from both of these experiences.

Laughter is God's gift to a troubled world. "Laugh lots," an elderly lady once told me, "and when you grow old all your wrinkles will be in the right places." How right she was! G.K. Chesterton called joy "the great note all through the Bible." The fiery preacher Billy Sunday once said, "If you have no joy, there's a leak in your Christianity somewhere." I like that.

Has joy been seeping from your life lately? Have circumstances crowded out the vibrancy of your walk with God? If so, let me remind you that some golf courses are full of cacti, but you don't need to sit on one.

Today you will be handed opportunities to get angry, to get even, to blame and pout, to hang onto grudges, or to tell somebody off. Use these moments to be thankful and forgiving, to overflow with joy.

"Always be joyful," wrote the apostle Paul in 1 Thessalonians 5:16-18, "keep on praying. No matter what happens, always be thankful, for this is God's will for you who belong to Christ Jesus."

Don't forget to try out a few practical jokes on the golf course. Be warned, though. If your wife is expecting, be careful when you laugh. And watch how much mustard you put on that mouse.

⚑

Thank You, Lord, for the gift of laughter.
Help me choose it over bitterness and anger today.
May Your joy be seen in the way I talk—
and even in the way I look today. Amen.

You shall have no other gods before me.
Exodus 20:3 NIV

19

Confessions of a Sports Nut

*"Talking to a golf ball won't do you any good.
Unless you do it while your opponent is teeing
off."*

—Bruce Lansky

I first got involved in organized sports back in fourth
grade when, because of federal law, I was forced to join
Organized Hockey. In Organized Hockey, we played a
game that closely resembled real ice hockey, except that
in real ice hockey, players skate around gracefully and
shoot the puck into the net. We did not do this. Instead,
we plowed headfirst into the boards, fell over one another,
and received so many concussions that we forgot things....
Now, let's see, where was I? Oh yes, now I remember...

I've had a love affair with sports all my life. If it
bounced, slid, rolled, or flew, I chased it. For many years,
sports became my obsession—my idol, if you will. I
immersed myself in statistics and scoreboards and would
sooner worship at the shrine of sport than anyplace else.

My friend Gord can attest to that. In those days the
two of us appeared to be normal and rational. But take us

to a golf course or a hockey arena and the "competition gene" kicked in, forcing us to go to almost any length to win. It wasn't always pretty, but on occasion it provided a little humor. Once, as I lined up an important putt, Gord whispered, "Those are nice pants, Phil. Too bad they didn't have your size." On the final hole I pointed out a mythical deer running toward the clubhouse, and when he looked, I stepped on his Top Flite ball, squashing it a quarter inch into the green. Gord lost by a single stroke that day. Two days later he was still scratching his head trying to figure out how he bounced an 8-inch putt.

My increasing obsession with sports brought out the worst in me. I didn't bow down and worship my golf clubs, but I came close. If given the choice between time with God or time on the course, I threw my clubs in the trunk. God used a simple phone call one day to change my priorities. It came when I called my golfing buddy. "You want me to beat you again, Gord?" I asked.

There was silence.

"I've...well...I've just been to see the doctor," he said. "I've had this scratchy throat for months, and it's been getting worse. The doctor says it looks like lymphoma, a rather deadly sort of cancer."

I didn't know what to say.

"When will you find out more?" I finally stammered.

"The results don't come back 'til Tuesday." Gord's voice was shaky. "I could tell by the doctor's face that the news won't be good."

I was silent for a minute. "I'm so sorry," I said at last. "Tell you what. If the news is the worst, I'll take you golfing anywhere you want. Anywhere."

"Australia?"

"You're on," I gulped.

"Will you let me beat you?"

"Absolutely," I chuckled. "I'll be praying."

The next week was one of the longest of my life. I lived on my knees, praying for Gord. I couldn't imagine golfing without my friend. And when I stood up from my knees, I knew I needed to do something else. Something I'd never done before. I gave my golf clubs to God. That sounds strange, I suppose. But I offered Him my obsession and asked Him to be number one in every area of my life.

"Lord," I prayed, "I don't want anything to take the place You were meant to be."

On Tuesday the phone rang. It was Gord.

"Bad news," he said.

I held my breath. *No...please, Lord—*

"I guess we don't get to golf in Australia," he laughed. "It's not as serious as we thought. I'll be fine!"

To celebrate, Gord and I golfed together. I can't remember who won. What mattered more was the conversation, the stories of our children, and our walk with God. Few rounds of golf have I enjoyed more than this one. I discovered a simple but profound truth that day: The things we clutch tightly, we lose. But whatever we place in God's hands, we will possess forever.

What occupies top spot in your life? Have you put it above God? It could be golf, a person, a car, a job, or a goal. Will you give it to Him today?

⚑

*Thank You, Lord, for giving me so many things
to enjoy. May none of them occupy the spot
You were meant to occupy. Amen.*

Pride goes before destruction,
a haughty spirit before a fall.
Proverbs 16:18 NIV

20

Downswing

"I'm the best. I just haven't played it yet."
—MUHAMMAD ALI, WHEN ASKED
ABOUT HIS GOLF GAME

One day, when I was eight years old, my father pulled up in our 1962 Ford Meteor and ceremoniously dislodged a well-worn set of Arnold Palmer/Ben Hogan/Heinz 57 clubs from the backseat. "You be careful with these, son," Dad warned me as I danced tight circles around those clubs. "I paid five dollars for them."

My eyes widened to think of that much money all in one place. "I'll be careful," I said. And for the most part, I was.

We lived in a tiny white house on the edge of town in those days. From its backyard I could tee up a ball and pound it 100 yards into a farmer's field (if a stiff wind was cheering for me). Then I'd run after it and do it again. My friends and I buried nine mushroom soup cans in that yard, open-side up, and plotted a course. Par was 27. I was happy. Life was good.

One day, however, golf took a swing for the worse. On that fateful day, my friend Stanley Kirk came over to admire my stroke and listen to me boast.

"I can hit farther than anyone my age," I told him. "Maybe in the *world*." I teed up a dimpled ball and told Stanley how accurate I was and that no one else in third grade at Prairie Elementary School could strike a ball as straight as I could, that I was probably "Going Somewhere Fast with Great Possibilities and Real Potential."

Then, as Stanley watched, I pulled a 1-wood from the bag, brought it back in a smooth arch, and swung like I'd never swung before. Trouble was, on the downswing I got more of Stanley than I got of the ball. To be specific, I hit him in the forehead. Turning in horror, the club still vibrating in my hands, I saw my former friend was standing there, stunned, blood running down the left side of his face. Until now, golf had been a noncontact sport for Stanley. He spent the day at the hospital. I spent it searching for that ball.

You don't have to look far in the wild world of sports to find boastful people like me, people with egos the size of Don King's hairdo. King, the fight promoter, once boasted, "I never cease to amaze myself. I say this humbly." Golfer Johnny Miller said, "I'm not sure that the most talented player I ever saw wasn't myself." Howard Cosell took it further, "There never has been one like me before," he said, "and there never will be one like me again." Baseball great Ted Williams told the media, "I can't stand it, I'm so good," and Baseball Hall of Famer Bo Belinsky took it even further: "My only regret," he said, "is that I can't sit in the stands and watch myself pitch."

Pride is a strange disease, isn't it? It makes everyone sick...except the person who has it! C.S. Lewis called pride "the great sin," the one that everyone hates to see in others, but can't imagine being guilty of themselves. Competitive by nature, pride derives no real pleasure from a great golf score—only from having a better score than the next guy. "Pride leads to disgrace," Proverbs 11:2 tells us, "but with humility comes wisdom."

> When Jack Fleck beat Ben Hogan in a playoff to win the 1955 U.S. Open, he was using a set of Ben Hogan golf clubs.

I don't know what a truly humble golfer would look like if I met him. I suppose he wouldn't boast about his swing, and he wouldn't know he was humble at all. Chances are, he would be a cheerful, intelligent part of our foursome, who would take more interest in us than we do in him. And if he did any bragging at all, it would be of only one thing: "The person who wishes to boast should boast only of what the Lord has done" (1 Corinthians 1:31).

More than 30 years have passed since Stanley and I tried out that 1-wood together. I'm more careful with my downswing now. And I'm glad to say that Stanley is still my friend today. But I never did find that ball.

Perhaps it rolled into one of those mushroom soup cans.

⚑

Dear Lord, forgive me for my foolish pride.
As long as I am looking down on others, I can't see
what's above me. Help me look to You, today. Amen.

You will keep in perfect peace all who trust in you,
whose thoughts are fixed on you.
Isaiah 26:3

21

Flagstick

"We learn so many things from golf—how to
suffer, for instance."

—BRUCE LANSKY

On the back nine of the Dinosaur Trail Golf and Country Club in Drumheller, Alberta, is one of the most irritating par fours on earth. Although it is only 307 yards from the silver tee markers to the center of the cup, there is no way of seeing where you are shooting. A white sign with an arrow points the way, but the best drive is merely a hopeful one. They call the surrounding area The Badlands, and for good reason. Steep cliffs, small cacti, and fanged rattlesnakes guard your ball should it stray into the rough. Dead dinosaurs are being unearthed nearby, and paleontologists don't appreciate interruptions. This past summer I launched three balls from the silver markers in the general direction of that arrow. I found only one of them and was forced to take an eight.

If you've ever golfed in a fog, you know the feeling. I've done it only once in my life, and I won't do it again. Someone yelled "fore" and I almost fell into a creek. Every single hole was a guessing game. The flagsticks, which hours earlier had provided a fixed target, had vanished into the mist.

The third hole on the course where I golfed as a child was a long one, up and over the brow of a steep hill that hid the flagstick from view. The only time I knew where I was going was when my father was with me. He stood tall, just tall enough to tell me where to aim. "See the top of that poplar tree to the left of the fencepost," he'd point. I would shake my head. "Here," he'd say, lifting me on his shoulders. And about 26 shots later I'd reach the hole.

Before the tragedy of September 11, 2001, people in the downtown area of New York navigated by the trade towers. "Everything is located in relationship to them," said one man, as he stood on the street, weeping. "We can't believe they're gone. We're simply disoriented."

Few things in this life remain constant, certain, unchanging. Some of my best friends have moved away in the past year. Two are now in heaven. Others have lost jobs or watched their health decline. Sometimes I long for those days when my father would put me on his shoulders and show me the direction to take. Life gets confusing. I have more questions than answers, it seems.

In the last decade, my wife's family has been devastated by Huntington's disease, a rare genetic disorder that causes mental and physical deterioration. Three of Ramona's siblings suffer from it. Miriam is one. Doctors who treat thousands of Huntington's patients are amazed at how slowly the disease is growing in her body. The reasons are numerous: a loving husband and family, a positive attitude that never ceases to amaze us, but most of all a calm assurance that comes from having Jesus as the one constant in her life. "It seems your belief in a higher power has helped you," a psychologist told Miriam and Jim one day.

Miriam smiled. "That would be God," she said.

Her simple, childlike trust is a quiet testimony to so many. For Miriam, life may be falling apart at the edges, but not at the core. At the very center, she knows she is loved by God, held in His arms, and promised the eternal joys of heaven. She can't always see the target, but she asks God for just enough light for the next shot.

Are circumstances making it tough for you to see the way? Remember, Jesus is that one navigational point that is indestructible!

Father, help me have a childlike faith during tough times.
Thank You for promising never to leave or forsake me.
I pray with the man in Mark 9:24,
"[Lord], I believe, but help me not to doubt." Amen.

We ask God to…make you wise with spiritual wisdom.
Then the way you live will always honor and please the Lord,
and you will continually do good, kind things for others.
Colossians 1:9-10

22

Simple Pleasures

*"They say that life is a lot like golf. Don't believe
them. Golf is a lot more complicated."*
—GARDNER DICKINSON

One of the joys of small-town living is the simple pleasure of lunch at home. Many weekends find me in large
cities speaking to large audiences, but when I drive back
to our sleepy little town of 4,000 (including cats), it's like
someone loosened my tie. I love the city; I love the people.
But I'm most at home here. Many days, at noon, I walk
five or six minutes, arriving at my front door in time to
kiss my wife. We sit together on the back porch munching
sandwiches, surveying the ripening wheat fields, and
talking about our children who are stuck at school.

If it sounds like Little House on the Prairie, it's not.
It's much better.

One day as I walked home past the schoolyard with
my wife's welcome kiss on my mind, I noticed my son's
class was hitting golf balls into a field under the watchful

gaze of the physical education instructor. The instructor, a friend of mine, called me over and challenged me to a duel with one of the students. Whoever hit their ball closest to an orange cone would be the recipient of a can of pop at the other's expense. He handed me a club that Noah used on the ark. I thought it was a wedge. It was an 8-iron.

My opponent launched a surprisingly accurate shot. Then it was my turn. I swung. And lost. Badly.

Walking home with my head down, I thought of some good excuses. I hadn't stretched. The club was old. *I* am old. Then came an idea. It would cost me ten dollars, delay lunch, and leave a few things undone. But walking home that day, I wondered how many more years my son would be standing among his classmates, watching his dad make a fool of himself, and perhaps feeling just a little bit proud of him for doing so.

Grabbing my wallet, I jumped into our van and drove to the grocery store. Half an hour later I pulled cans from a cooler full of ice and watched a class of 23 gulp a 24-pack of soda in record time. "Thanks, Mr. Callaway," they kept saying, "that was cool."

As my wife and I sat on the back deck later, I noted that it doesn't take much to make someone's day. A kind word. A short note. A loaf of homemade bread. A can of soda. Too often we Christians think we must do or say something philosophical or weighty to have an impact for the kingdom. We don't. More often, the most profound act is a simple one. A thoughtful word to the one pumping gas may bring sunshine to a cloudy day. A compliment to the lady who takes our green fee or drives the refreshment cart just might turn her day around. The fast-paced and greedy world in which we live does not encourage such activities. God's Word does. "Clothe yourselves with tenderhearted mercy, kindness, humility, gentleness, and patience," we are instructed in Colossians 3:12,14, "…and the most important piece of clothing you must wear is love."

"Kindness," a very wise man once said, "has converted more sinners than zeal, eloquence, or learning." Perhaps he was right.

Like you, I have some regrets in life. The soda adventure is not one of them. But I would like to shoot that 8-iron again. I think I could get it closer to the cone this time.

⚑

Dear Father, help me recognize the opportunities
for kindness that intersect my path each day.
Help me remember that one kind act
can speak louder than 100 sermons. Amen.

The LORD opens the eyes of the blind....
The LORD loves the righteous.
Psalm 146:8

23

Leading the Blind

"Learn from the skillful. He who teaches him-
self hath a fool for his master."
—BEN FRANKLIN

The third hole on our town's small course is a frustrating par five that requires binoculars on the tee-box if you hope to see the flagstick. People sometimes begin their round with great expectations, peaceful thoughts, and kind words for their fellow man, but by the time they reach the green on number 3, they are writing a classified ad: "Clubs. Cheap. Used once too often." The sloping green is protected by water behind and before, and the fairway is a paper-thin stripe parting two thirsty creeks. To reach the 150-yard markers, I require a laser beam 1-wood, followed by a perfect 5-iron. At times, I try a fairway wood on my second shot and hope for the best, but I'm learning that greed and good golf seldom coexist.

My brother, Dan, and I, together with our sons, stood atop the third tee-box recently, avoiding the urge to laugh at one another. My nephew Bradley has a hook you could catch trout with. It sometimes finds other fairways...and other zip codes. He has inherited this hook from his dad. Following their tee shots both of them turned to me and asked for advice. "I think you're dropping your front shoulder," I said. "You're bringing your back arm around too far. Maybe try to keep your front arm straighter...your follow-through is all wrong."

Then I stepped up to the tee and sliced a brand-new Callaway ball into the creek 50 yards to the right. It was Dan and Bradley's turn to offer me advice. "You dropped your shoulder," joked Bradley. "I think it's your follow-through," said Dan. There was nothing left to do but laugh. And hit provisional balls.

Funny, isn't it? The less skillful the player, the more likely he is to offer advice.

In Matthew 15:14, Jesus refers to the Pharisees as blind guides: "If a blind man leads a blind man, both will fall into a pit" (NIV). I picture Peter on a driving range trying to fix the other disciples' hooks before slicing his own shot over the fence to the right. The Master is nearby grinning. Perhaps that's why Jesus elaborated in Luke 6:42: "How can you think of saying, 'Friend, let me help you get rid of that speck in your eye,' when you can't see past the log in your own eye? First get rid of the log from your own eye; then perhaps you will see well enough to deal with the speck in your friend's eye."

> Odds an amateur golfer will score a hole in one: 43,000 to 1.

As surely as we consult the right book or the right golf pro to fix our swing, so we must look to the right source for direction in life. Twenty-one times in the Gospels Jesus says, "Follow me." In Isaiah 42:16, God promises,

I will lead the blind by ways they have not
known, along unfamiliar paths I will guide them;
I will turn the darkness into light before them
and make the rough places smooth. These are
the things I will do; I will not forsake them
(NIV).

Comforting words to golfers. We've all experienced
"unfamiliar paths." We've needed darkness turned to light
and wished the rough was made smooth.

Only one teacher can do that.

Psalm 146:8 promises that "the LORD gives sight to
the blind, the LORD lifts up those who are bowed down,
the LORD loves the righteous" (NIV).

Whose "swing" are you following today?

*Thank You, Lord, that You give sight to the blind,
lift up those who humble themselves, and love the unlovely.
Help me to watch who I follow, to choose carefully
my words of advice, and to never stop looking to You
when my sight grows dim. Amen.*

Let us aim for harmony in the church
and try to build each other up.
Romans 14:19

24

The Last Tee Time

"Focus on remedies, not faults."
—JACK NICKLAUS

On a list of my favorite golfing buddies, Cordell Darling ranks high. Last June, along with about 80 other golfers, we attended a tournament at a beautiful lakeside course not far from home. Cordell was one of the sponsors; I was the speaker. Prizes were passed out, including clubs, balls, bags, and more balls. Names were drawn from a broad-brimmed hat. Cordell's insurance company donated three prizes. Incredibly, he won two of them. His son won the other. I kid you not. "Next year, I bet you'll donate a Mercedes," I said to Cordell as I took the podium. I can still hear his infectious chuckle.

Two weeks later, as I came in the door, my wife put an arm around me. "I have bad news," she said. "Cordell is gone. Killed in a car accident." I slumped to the floor in disbelief. "No," was all I could manage. My friend. One of my biggest encouragers. Gone. It couldn't be.

Exactly two weeks earlier we had been at the golf course, joking about his prizes, talking about our swings. Now he was home, claiming the real prize.

The world slows down remarkably when a friend dies. Things you once thought important don't mean a thing. Things you worried about yesterday vanish today. Money won't buy what you want, and sometimes you find yourself wishing for five more minutes to say what you didn't say when you know you should have.

Cordell didn't leave things unsaid. He would meet you in the foyer of our church with welcome written on his face and encouragement on his lips. Some consider it their spiritual gift to complain about the music, or the hairdos, or the sermon. Cordell would tell you how wonderful things were. Some delight in pointing fingers at the world. Cordell told you what God was doing there. "Awesome" was one of his favorite words. "Fabulous" was another. Cordell read Scripture verses, then went out and practiced their truths.

Sometimes you can measure a man's influence by the volume of cigarette butts in the church parking lot at his funeral. There were plenty at this one. Fifteen hundred people don't show up to much in a small town, but that many gathered to say goodbye to one of my favorite golfers. Many were "pre-Christians," as Cordell loved to call them. Dozens considered him their best friend. As a member of what the insurance world calls the Million Dollar Round Table, Cordell had experienced much of what we call success. But he always seemed to have time for people. He was my high school hockey coach, my cheerleader, and one of my biggest fans.

"Who makes a humorist laugh?" someone once asked me. "Guys like Cordell," I replied.

"My father was part Scotch," he had jokingly told me over a glass of Pepsi a week before his death, "part Ginger Ale."

When we left for the funeral, I told my sons I would pay them a dime for every adjective they wrote down that was used to described Cordell. Their pockets are jingling now. "He loved God," Stephen wrote. "Comforter. Encourager. Servant. Honest in business. Enjoyed life. Loved his grandkids. Loved golf."

When my wife and I were first married, Cordell took us out for lunch, hoping to sell us life insurance. And he told us that no matter what our decision, the very best life insurance policy wasn't for sale. The assurance that we can live forever with Jesus by simple faith in God is the best present we'll ever receive, and it was free for the asking. That message has changed our focus, our direction, our very lives.

I wish for every church a Cordell, for every community, every home, and every golf course. If something blessed him, he said so. He was human like the rest of us, but he kept pointing us higher. Cordell's golf swing needed some work, but it wasn't that important to him. He was too busy encouraging others or praying for them.

He never met anyone who was just plain ordinary. They were fantastic, unbelievable, or incredible. Cordell used exclamation marks when he described you. He looked past my faults and embellished my attributes. To him I didn't have a slice, I had "a creative way of allowing my ball to see maximum yardage and scenery."

A few months ago Cordell sat in my office. "I'm learning to slow down," he said. "To squeeze the day. Six grandchildren help you do that."

"Let's get together soon...maybe do some golfing" were Cordell's last words to me.

One day soon I'll keep that tee time. I can hardly wait.

⚑

Lord, help me see what You are doing in others and point it out to them. Help me catch people doing something right and tell them about it. Thank You for the "Cordells" in my life. May I lift others up by pointing them to You. Amen.

*Your word is a lamp for my feet
and a light for my path.*
Psalm 119:105

25

Absolutes

*"One of the advantages bowling has over golf
is that you seldom lose a bowling ball."*
—DON CARTER, PROFESSIONAL BOWLER

My son's teacher called one night. "Uh oh," I said to my wife, cupping my hand over the phone. But this time was different. This time the teacher wanted a favor. "Would you come teach our PE class the basics of golf? After all, your name is Callaway." Out of sheer gratitude that my son had not cut off someone's pigtail or put Superglue on the principal's chair, I said yes.

A week later, I found myself on the driving range with 20 noisy tenth-graders and no megaphone. Gathering them in a loose circle, I started with a brief discussion of golf etiquette and demonstrated how to repair a divot and grip the club so as not to injure golfers on other fairways. Then I showed them the basic stance and how to attain a sweet swing that will cause the sky to look bluer and galleries to request your autograph. I threw in a generous dose of humor, hoping to excite them about this great game.

The response was surprising. A few showed genuine interest. Most, understandably, wanted to hurry up and try it out for themselves. Three young ladies asked if they could go get a drink (I pointed them to the creek). One held a club like a pool cue. Another dropped about 20 balls and began hitting them in rapid succession like a machine gun, moving healthy chunks of real estate and scattering balls everywhere. I approached him and explained a few things. He looked at me and shrugged.

"Whatever," he said. I smiled and shook my head.

In 1962, Jack Nicklaus made his debut on the PGA tour at the Los Angeles Open...and finished last.

We live in a "whatever" world, don't we? Whatever is good at the time. Whatever gets us through. But golf is not a "whatever" sport. Golf, by nature, is a precision game where the rules, the stance, and the swing very much matter. As in life, a "whatever" attitude will get us absolutely nowhere. There is a right way to golf and a wrong way. The right way provides pleasure. The wrong way spells disaster. So it is in life. Children raised in a society that has rejected the notions of absolute truth and morality will have trouble with more than their golf swings.

On a plane recently, my wife and I found ourselves seated beside two college students who, unprompted, began talking about religion. "I'm sort of a Buddhist, but sort of, like, a Christian, you know," said Mike, a wide-eyed 19-year-old. "I kind of like Hinduism, too. Most of the big religions are sort of cool. They all have trinities, our professor says." His live-in girlfriend nodded, twirling a cross necklace. "Whatever works," she said.

Mike turned to me. "So what religion are you?"

"I'm not into religion," I told him. "I just have a relationship with Jesus. He's changed everything."

"Oh," he said, "Jesus is cool. He was a good teacher. So was Mohammed."

"Well, I used to think that too, Mike," I said. "But Jesus can't just be a good teacher."

"What do you mean?"

"Well, if your religion professor came to class one day and said, 'I have an announcement to make: I'm the Son of God. I'm the way, the truth, and the life, no one comes to God except through me,' what would you think?"

"I'd think he was crazy," said Mike. Then he paused and wrinkled his brow. I watched a light come on. "Oh," he muttered softly, "I see what you mean."

"Jesus claimed to be the Son of God, Mike. Either He was lying, or He was crazy, or He was right. You have to choose. They didn't crucify Him because He was a nice guy or a good teacher. As C.S. Lewis said, 'Either He was a liar, a lunatic, or He was Lord.'"

Beside me, my wife's head was bowed.

"I think I know the answer." Mike said, quietly nodding his head. "He must be Lord."

That day, before exiting the plane, we exchanged addresses so I could send Mike and his girlfriend Bibles. And I told them that if my wife starts praying for them, they won't have a chance. Smiling, they said they wouldn't mind at all if she did.

Such a message stands in sharp contrast in a "whatever" world—in a society that has dethroned the notions of absolute truth and morality. But as surely as your golf stroke will deteriorate if you ignore certain laws, so your spirit will wither without careful attention to God's laws.

Do you have a "whatever" attitude toward life? Or a deep and abiding love for God's Word, His character, and His purposes?

Much more than your golf swing is at stake.

⚑

Lord, guide my steps by Your Word,
so I will not be overcome by any evil. Amen.
(See Psalm 119:13.)

"For I know the plans I have for you,"
declares the LORD, "plans to prosper you
and not to harm you, plans to
give you hope and a future."
Jeremiah 29:11 NIV

26

Mountaintop Golfing

"I'd rather be a poor winner than any kind of
loser."

—GEORGE S. KAUFMAN
PLAYWRIGHT AND SPORTS FAN

If you've ever watched the final round of the Masters or another prestigious golf event on television, chances are you flipped the TV off before the trophy was presented. But if you did, you missed something. Most fans linger after the match—not for the sponsor's words, but for the champion's thoughts.

What separated him or her from hundreds of other golfers?

What did it feel like to sink that winning putt?

Many credit a particular club, the course, or a caddy. Some mention their psychiatrist or a lucky bounce or two. "I was too scared to look," joked one winner, "so I just closed my eyes and swung." Lately I've heard a number of champions give thanks to God or their relationship with Jesus Christ, recognizing that all good things come from

Him. Tom Lehman, British Open Champ, PGA Player of the Year, and Vardon Trophy Winner, is quick to credit God, calling the Christian life "the greatest of all challenges." Veterans like Bernhard Langer and Paul Azinger also speak openly of their faith.

Equally interesting to me is the interview with the second- and third-place finishers. Usually their heads are slightly lowered and their tone soft and apologetic. "I just didn't have it out there today," they often say, shrugging, "I left it in the bag." Sometimes they are less gracious, blaming a caddy, an official, or the weather. Off camera, some have been known to throw things in disgust and use words they didn't learn in Sunday school.

But of all the responses I've heard, I'm still waiting for this one from a losing golfer: "You know, I just wanna thank God for this loss." Wouldn't we sit up straight on that one? What if he or she continued, "I love winning tournaments, but I don't seem to grow much when everything is going my way. I seem to learn life's biggest lessons during the toughest times. I guess shattered dreams are God's unexpected gateway to joy."

Wouldn't that be something? Wouldn't that be perceptive?

Tell me, when was the last time you grew through success? It's pretty rare, isn't it. But have you grown through difficulty? I have. In fact, I don't seem to grow any other way.

We live a few short hours from the Rocky Mountains and some of the most beautiful golf courses on the globe. But none of them are built near the majestic mountain peaks. Rocks abound up there, but water does not. It is down in the valley where the

> To train Tommy Nakajima to play in the rain, his father used to squirt him in the face with a hose while the future pro hit golf balls.

river flows that we find the tall pines, the lush grass, and the narrow fairways.

So it is in life.

We all love mountaintop experiences, but we don't grow there. Life's larger lessons are learned most often through tough times.

There are approximately 400 dimples on the average golf ball. Have you ever wondered how a golf ball would fly without them? I'm told a dimpleless golf ball will fly about 60 to 80 yards, taking off like an ordinary ball, then dropping quickly to earth. (I hope that doesn't sound like your drive.) Without those little divots, the ball would be useless.

As surely as a golf ball needs those indentations, the trials of life deepen us and put our character to the test. Those difficult times can bring out the worst in us, but when we choose joy, embrace courage, and follow Christ, they can help us discover the very best God has for us.

The trials of life also prepare us to help those who are experiencing difficulty. Second Corinthians 1:4 teaches that "[God] comforts us in all our troubles so that we can comfort others." Have you found yourself in the school of difficulty lately? If so, may I share with you two verses that have been of great comfort to me when the valley has closed in?

> For our present troubles are quite small and won't last very long. Yet they produce for us an immeasurably great glory that will last forever! So we don't look at the troubles we can see right now; rather, we look forward to what we have not yet seen. For the troubles we see will soon

be over, but the joys to come will last forever
(2 Corinthians 4:17-18).

*Lord, I do not pray for difficulty, but for enough strength
for each day. May I be a comfort to others,
just as You have comforted me. Amen.*

Teach us to number our days aright,
that we may gain a heart of wisdom.
Psalm 90:12 NIV

27

The Real Thing

"Every day on the golf course is about making
little adjustments, taking what you've got on
that day and finding the way to deal with it."
—TIGER WOODS

Today, as I sat in my office writing this book, the phone rang: "Dad," said my 15-year-old son Stephen, "what are you doing?"

I told him.

He was unimpressed. "Come on," he urged. "It's beautiful outside. Let's go golfing."

From my window, July beckoned. The temperature was perfect. The sun, hidden from view yesterday, was out in full, drying the grass and extending golfers a perfect prospect.

"How can I go?" I thought aloud. "I'm staring down the barrel of a deadline. I'm speaking at a large convention this weekend."

"I better not, son," I heard myself say.

"All right," was his gracious response before hanging up.

A story comes to mind.

A simple story that makes me wonder...

On Monday, October 25, 1999, Danny De Armas learned that famous golfer Payne Stewart's plane had gone down in South Dakota, killing all aboard.

It hit closer to home than you can imagine.

Four days earlier, at home in Florida, Danny had received a phone call from Van Arden, the father of his son's best friend, Ivan. "Hey," he said, "it's my forty-fifth birthday. Let's take Ivan and your son Seth out of school and go golfing."

Unfortunately, Danny had to decline. He was traveling the next morning to California and life had been a little hectic lately. So Van offered to take the boys himself. Danny hoped to take them golfing someday too, but not today. And so the boys helped Van celebrate his birthday with a day of golf at the Grand Cypress Resort. It was Ivan's favorite thing to do with his dad.

"It was a blast," Seth said later. He ended up spending Friday and Saturday night at the Ardens' home. They rode go-peds and skateboards. They even built a kid-made, three-hole golf course in the front yard.

The following Monday, golfer Payne Stewart, known for his signature knickers, climbed aboard a Lear jet headed for Dallas. The passengers aboard were Payne and five others— including his agent...Ivan's dad.

On Tuesday morning, Danny arrived back in Orlando. Seth told him that Ivan wanted to get out of the house for a while, because there were too many people around, and he needed some space. So that afternoon Danny took the boys golfing. "It was my first chance to see the two of them on the golf course together," he says. "It was about time." As they played, they talked about Van's slice and how he loved to let the boys drive the carts. They talked about life and death. And friendship.

On the way home, Danny choked back tears as the boys read aloud 30 cards Ivan had received from his friends at school. The car was filled with laughter as the boys admired the artwork of their friends. Each card tried in some way to ease the pain Ivan was feeling.

That night as Danny lay in bed, he contemplated his friend's death. It was a startling reminder that we may not have much to offer others, but we can give them our time.

Most people I know don't need another guilt trip, but at times we need a wake-up call. I have yet to meet someone whose final wish was that he could spend a little more time with his newspaper. Or his computer. Or his television set. But I have met too many who seem to be spending the last half of their lives regretting the first half. Unfortunately, time doesn't take time off, it slips through our fingers like last month's paycheck. It's not an easy balance, I know. We must make money to make a living. We also must make memories to make a life.

I am not the sharpest knife in the drawer, but I'm smart enough to know that my son won't be calling me forever to say, "Let's go golfing, Dad." "Time waits for no man," says my father, "and very few women!" And so, if it's okay with you, I will finish this paragraph and shut down the computer. Then I'll call my son. I'll tell him that writing about golf is fun, but it's a pale substitute for the real thing.

⚑

Lord, help me spend my time on nothing I should have to
repent of or for which I cannot ask Your blessing.
Give me the wisdom to balance the demands of a busy life
with the opportunities to impact eternity.
Thank You for those who will cry at my funeral,
and for the opportunity to hang out with them. Amen.

*A man's life does not consist in the
abundance of his possessions.*
Jesus, Luke 12:15 NIV

28

Accessories

*"To be truthful, I think golfers are overpaid.
It's unreal, and I have trouble dealing with
the guilt sometimes."*

—COLIN MONTGOMERIE

Can you believe how much stuff is out there that relates to golf? We've got Three Stooges golf mugs, golf books for dummies, shaving kits for duffers, and shoebags, wallets, and underwear for everyone else. You can hardly open your car door anymore without hitting a golf accessory. How did a sport that rewards the person who does the least, manage to clutter itself with so much?

The answer, we both know, is money. And there's plenty to go around. Want some sterling silver golf cufflinks so you can check the temperature of your wrists before each putt? They're available for $98. As I write this, a 1996 Tiger Woods rookie card, which the seller insists is "the single greatest treasure in existence," could be mine for a cool $600,000.

A hundred times a day advertisers bombard our minds to create necessities for us, remind us we are unhappy, tell us we don't have enough, and encourage us to do something about it. "You do not have clubs like these ones," the advertisers say. "You don't drive a car like the one Tiger is in, you poor soul." "You do not watch golf on a television as large as this one, or vacation at a huge golf resort where your children surround you on the beach at night, bringing you drinks and laughing at all your jokes."

I think we could take a lesson from the game of golf. In golf, the one with the lowest score wins.

We've all heard golfers say, "I got my money's worth today," meaning that if they were paying by the stroke, they got quite a deal. But ask most golfers if they would trade a score that resembles their bowling game for a 72, and they will take you up on it.

> Amateur golfers average a 97 for 18 holes.

Wouldn't that be refreshing to see in life?

We live in a culture that encourages big numbers at the end of the game. "He who dies with the most toys wins," boasts a bumper sticker. "How much was he worth?" people whisper in the back row at the funeral parlor. But money is a lousy way of keeping score. It seems to me that the one who dies with the most toys loses more than the next guy. It's the one who gives his life away who wins in the end. That's what Christ did for us. "Though he was very rich, yet for your sakes he became poor, so that by his poverty he could make you rich" (2 Corinthians 8:9).

Clarence Strom was my pastor when I was a boy. He was a devout, unselfish, gentle servant of God. On his deathbed, Mr. Strom was surrounded by family who ushered him into heaven, singing hymns and praising God for his simple life. The same week I attended Mr. Strom's funeral, I heard from a man who stood by his father's deathbed where bitter relatives fought over his large estate. That battle continues to this day. Does the man with the most toys really win?

Paul's words to Timothy are blunt and well worth meditating on:

> Tell those rich in this world's wealth to quit being so full of themselves and so obsessed with money, which is here today and gone tomorrow. Tell them to go after God, who piles on all the riches we could ever manage—to do good, to be rich in helping others, to be extravagantly generous. If they do that, they'll build a treasury that will last, gaining life that is truly life (1 Timothy 6:17-19 THE MESSAGE).

Jesus challenged us to "store up for yourselves treasures in heaven, where moth and rust do not destroy, and where thieves do not break in and steal" (Matthew 6:20 NIV). Obedience to Christ means choosing the way of the cross. It is the way of giving, not taking. Of contentment, not consumption. Of receiving the lowest score, and winning.

Don't get me wrong. As Christians, we are free to enjoy things. But possessions must never own us. Are you cluttering your life with the latest golf accessories? Can you laugh at the crazy ones without buying them?

Remember, real wealth is not determined by what we accumulate, but by what we embrace. We can tell more about a person by what he gives away than by what he leaves behind.

Lord, help me to neither be a prisoner of stuff nor a prisoner of envy. Give me an eternal perspective and daily reminders of the things that will last. Amen.

Plans fail for lack of counsel,
but with many advisors they succeed.
Proverbs 15:22 NIV

29

Foursome

"Have you ever noticed what golf spells backward?"
—AL BOLISKA

I was ten when I discovered that some people don't like golf. I chipped a brand-new ball through my neighbor's window—and she kept it. To her, *golf* became a four-letter word. Perhaps it still is.

I know it's hard to believe, but some people hate the game. They don't like it. They won't play it. They don't get it. And don't ask them why because they just might tell you. For them, golf is people with badly mismatched clothing pushing dimpled balls around a perforated cow pasture while arguing about mathematics. They would sooner bang their heads with a bunker rake than golf.

I'm the opposite. I could golf every day if my wife encouraged me and brought the sandwiches. I suppose I golf partly to escape. It is almost impossible to remember how terrible the world is when you're gripping a 6-iron and staring at a magnificently manicured green surrounded by still waters. In a few hours you must return to the real world with its "to do lists" and many tragedies, but for now the golf course provides a badly needed respite.

Another reason I love the game of golf is the accountability.

If you've tried to get on a golf course by yourself lately, you know that very few courses let you go it alone. This is, of course, a financial decision, but it benefits more than the owners. Some years ago, I made the decision to take a friend or family member along when I fly to a strange city. Most often I take someone who loves to golf. The golf course is a safe place for us both (until someone yells "fore!"). I golf with friends not just because I have to, or because I love to, but because we were created to be in a circle of community. Golf, I suppose, has kept me from far greater sins. The golf course is one of the few places left that still seems to encourage accountability. Golfing with friends may lighten our wallet, but it also multiplies our joys and halves our sorrows.

One of the greatest losses our culture has experienced is the loss of community. We are self-sufficient now. We arrive home from work and pull into our garage without so much as a wave to the neighbor. We log on or grab the remote, all the while relishing anonymity and withdrawing from much-needed interaction, visibility, and vulnerability. Golf changes that. Though we keep track of our own score (some of us better than others), most golfers don't fly solo.

Recently I spent time on the phone with one of my favorite authors, Gordon MacDonald. His bestseller

Ordering Your Private World has shaped my life and thousands of others for the good. But a dozen years ago, Gordon's private world fell apart when he was involved in an affair. I asked him what he would have done differently. His response is well worth taping to the clubhouse mirror: "We have bought into the culture of individualism. Each of us is a solo performer. But what helps people survive and thrive is the accountability, support, and rebuke that comes from being in a tightly knit group. I need men in my life who will look me square in the eye and say, 'Gordon, at this point, you're full of it.' If I had that kind of friend ten years ago, we wouldn't be talking about failure today."

In 2 Corinthians 8 we read that the churches appointed Titus to accompany Paul as he transported money to Jerusalem. I don't know if they golfed along the way, but Paul did say words every golfer needs to hear today: "By traveling together we will guard against any suspicion, for we are anxious that no one should find fault with the way we are handling this generous gift. We are careful to be honorable before the Lord, but we also want everyone else to know we are honorable" (verses 20-21).

How about you? Are you a Lone Ranger Christian? Or are you traveling the course of this life with the support, the rebuke, and the advice of others? You will find safety in visibility, strength in numbers, and joy in accountability.

Lord, deliver me from the fear of being open before others.
Guide me to "a foursome" of those who would encourage me
in my walk with You. Amen.

*For though a righteous man falls
seven times, he rises again, but the wicked are
brought down by calamity.*
Proverbs 24:16

30

Sand Traps

*"Golf is a game in which you yell 'fore,' shoot
six, and write down five."*

—PAUL HARVEY

When I was a kid I couldn't sit still long enough to watch golf on TV. It looked slow—agonizingly slow. Watching cheese mold in the kitchen looked more exciting.

I loved hockey, but baseball, golf, and gymnastics bored me to tears. Unless it was full-contact gymnastics. All that changed, however, and today I love the tension of the final three holes. Or a playoff among the palm trees like the one I watched last week. But I have something to confess. I hope you won't think me a terrible person for it. Here goes. When I see seasoned veterans blow it, I am greatly encouraged. It's not that I'm cheering against them, it's just that they suddenly seem human—like me. When professionals hit water hazards, they may experience dejection, but they give me hope.

That's one of the things I love about the Bible. It's full of stories of saints who hit sand traps and landed out of play. Take Moses, for instance. The Egyptians found him in a huge water hazard (the Nile River), not knowing that he would one day lead all their employees away. But Moses didn't want the job. He stuttered. He stammered. He was weak in the knees. And Moses wasn't alone in Scripture. Abraham was a liar. David liked rooftops. Paul was a murderer, and Matthew worked for the IRS. But they all shared one thing in common: When they fell, they got back up. When they hit water hazards, they dropped another ball and took another swing. And God used them in mighty ways. Kind of gives us hope, doesn't it?

The first golfer that we know about in the Bible is the apostle Paul, whom theologians believe had about a 30 handicap. Though there is some debate on this, I believe they are right. Listen to Paul's words from the Callaway Revised Edition: "But one thing I do: Forgetting what happened at the last hole I look forward to what lies ahead, I press on toward the goal to win the prize of the upward call of God in Christ Jesus." (See Philippians 3:13.) Yes, I've taken certain liberties with the translation, but I believe Paul would agree.

If you ever wondered whether God can use someone like you, there are a thousand reasons around you to have hope.

Sunday mornings of my childhood were spent in church, listening to great preachers, singing wonderful hymns, and dreaming of the golf course. I was an earnest child. I wanted God to use me. But I knew He couldn't. After all, I had failed so often. When I looked at the preachers and hymn writers, they seemed to be on another spiritual plane altogether. They were like those pro golfers, and I held them in awe.

Once a month, during communion, we sang a marvelous hymn by William Cowper. I still remember the words: "There is a fountain filled with blood drawn from Emmanuel's veins. And sinners plunged beneath that flood lose all their guilty stains." I didn't know the author had hit his share of bunkers in life. Nor did I know that his story would one day give me hope.

William Cowper, who wrote these words of grace and assurance, was plagued by insecurity throughout his troubled life. Cowper suffered a nervous breakdown at one point, attempted suicide several times, and was even confined to an insane asylum and straight-jacketed for his own protection. Throughout his difficult life, he was haunted by the fear that God would one day turn His back on him. On his deathbed, however, it is said that William Cowper looked upward with amazement on his face and said, "I am not shut out of heaven after all."

The words of his hymns have comforted and encouraged Christians around the globe for centuries, offering hope to people like me who have struck out, doubted, and failed, but long for the day we will see our Savior face-to-face.

Lord, help me never underestimate what You can do through the most unlikely of people. Thank You for these stories of hope. Thank You for loving me and using me when I commit my failures to You and press on. Amen.

Teach your children to choose the right path, and when they are older, they will remain upon it.
Proverbs 22:6

31

Walk with Me

"A man leaves all kinds of footprints....Some you can see...others are invisible, like the prints he leaves across other people's lives."
—MARGARET RUNBECK

This past May, my son Stephen turned 15. My wife and I now have three teenagers. We need more prayer. We need more money. A week before his party, I asked my firstborn son what he could possibly want for his birthday considering that he already had me. He didn't pause or even laugh.

"Golf clubs," he said.

"How about something that doesn't cost any money?" I suggested.

He wouldn't hear of it.

So I started looking, and I found some right away. At a garage sale. The bag said ten dollars, but the owner assured me that no reasonable offer would be refused. I asked Stephen what he thought. He told me, "They were best before 1983, Dad."

So I kept looking. I found some Callaway golf clubs. My great uncle Eli, 13 times removed, owned the company before he passed away. And none of his offspring would return my mail. The clubs start at $2,500. Then you need a $700 driver and a $100 putter, and you should probably buy a matching bag, some funny-looking pants, and a few tees. Of course, I couldn't afford this, but a few days before the birthday, I managed to uncover a fabulous deal on a brand-new set of Wilsons—one I would have given my left arm for as a kid.

When Stephen ripped the wrapping off that Thursday, I had to peel him from the ceiling. I wouldn't have missed the expression on his face for anything.

"I didn't think you would—" he said.

"I didn't think I would either," I said.

"Let's try them out," we said together.

Since my son was four years old, we've walked hundreds of miles together on the golf course. Some people connect over fishing poles or stock cars or woodworking. For us, it's golf. I hope this doesn't sound trite, but I thank God for the game of golf. About twice a week, Stephen and I find ourselves talking about things we didn't intend to as we walk side by side down to the creek to look for my ball. We talk of music. And movies. And girls. And best of all, sometimes we find ourselves talking about Jesus—the third member of our threesome who has been beside us all these years. And I tell Stephen that I don't care if he makes a ton of money or becomes Prime Minister of Canada or the CEO of AOL.com, but if he walks with Jesus, I will be the most thankful guy alive.

"I have no greater joy," said the apostle John, "than to hear that my children are walking in the truth" (3 John 1:4 NIV). I understand how he felt.

I'm not as young as I once was. My children remind me of this sometimes. They're now at the age where they can almost take me in an arm wrestle or a sprint to the ice cream stand. I can't keep up with them in hockey much longer. I can't run circles around them in soccer like I used to. And riding a stair machine together is not much fun. But the one thing I'll be able to do with my sons long into old age (the Lord willing) is golf. All my life I've loved sports. Most pale in comparison with the longevity of a game played with a ball, some funny-looking sticks, and each other. Enduring, bonding activities are those that challenge, frustrate, surprise, and, in the end, leave us standing there together with a smile.

In 1457, the Scottish Parliament banned golf. It felt the time would be better spent practicing archery for the country's defense.

Let's not wait for a birthday or a new set of clubs to walk with the ones we love.

⚑

*Thank You, Lord, that You long to walk and talk
with us through the good times, through the tough times,
and all the way home. Amen.*

We are eagerly waiting for him to return
as our Savior. He will take these weak mortal bodies of ours
and change them into glorious bodies like his own.
Philippians 3:20

32

The Final Hole

*"A ball that rolls into an open grave may be
removed without penalty."*

—SIGN ON A GOLF COURSE THAT
RUNS THROUGH A GRAVEYARD
IN TIENTSIN, CHINA.

A book is never really finished, just abandoned. So many more stories linger, so many more thoughts come to mind. I've said them the best I can, but tomorrow I will think of a better way, I'm sure. I was going to tell you about more golfers I've known. About Paul Steinhauer, for instance. Almost every time I take a swing I think of my Californian friend. It's impossible not to. Paul gave me my clubs—a gorgeous set of Tour Legends that provide great pleasure but leave me few excuses. Paul left me far more than those clubs. He was the first friend I ever had who faced me with the truth of my own selfishness, hammered home some of the things you've read in this book, and catapulted me toward a deeper walk with God.

The last time we golfed together, we left the score-card in the clubhouse. A week earlier, Paul and his wife,

Judy, laid their only child to rest in a grave on the wind-swept prairies. Janella was the victim of a car crash. Paul just wanted to walk that day. The golf course seemed the ideal place for it. I didn't say much; I just listened.

"I don't know how I can go on," he told me, as he stood over a ball holding a 6-iron. "Janella would want me to keep going, I guess. To shoot again. Then walk toward the flagstick. You can't play all 18 holes at once." After a dreadful shot, Paul turned to me with a grin. "She would also want me to give you these clubs," he said.

I told him I couldn't take them. He said I had no choice.

"I just ordered a better set," he said. And for some reason we stood there laughing in the face of the worst tragedy we'd ever known.

I was going to tell you about the time I was robbed on the golf course. Not by a masked man on a golf cart, but by a more unusual suspect. My son and I were out with one of my best buddies, James Enns. On the seventh hole, a 527-yard par five, James and I both hit the green with our third shots. As we walked toward the hole with birdies on our minds, a large raven descended from the sky and landed on the green. Then, as you've already guessed, the bird took flight with James' golf ball in its beak. It flapped out of sight, then returned for mine. Neither of us knew the rules for such a predicament. We only knew that life is not fair—and sometimes golf isn't either.

A few months later, reality hit much harder. After a basketball game at Faith Academy in the Philippines,

James' nephew Stephen collapsed and died of heart failure. He was 17.

⚑

I was going to tell you about the sleepy Sunday afternoon when my own son Stephen was five years old. We drove past the graveyard where Janella and Stephen Enns would be buried many years later. Noticing a large pile of dirt beside a newly excavated tomb, Stephen pointed and said a most amazing and perceptive thing. "Look, Dad!" he said. "One got out!"

I laughed, but the more I think about it, the more I hang on to his words. You see, every time I pass a graveyard, every time I see a cross at the front of the church, I am reminded of those three words: *One got out*. That is the reason we can take that next shot. That is the reason we can keep walking toward the goal.

I don't have the answers for a friend of mine diagnosed with brain cancer weeks ago. I don't know what to say to the couple in our church who just lost a child. But those three words keep coming back to me.

"One got out."

Death could not keep our Savior in the ground. Jesus Christ, the one exception to all the rules, broke the chains of death, rose from the dead, and promised us eternity with Him. It is the central point of human history and the primary focus of all who embrace the Savior, who spread His arms wide on a Roman cross one awful day more than 2,000 years ago. There was nothing good about that Friday. It left 11 disciples in agony and His followers devastated. It was also mind-boggling. Perhaps they locked themselves away, asking questions no one could answer. Until that glorious Sunday when One got out. When the heart broken by our sin began to beat once again.

Such a thought is the most fitting conclusion for any book.

One day soon, those arms will spread wide again, welcoming us home. Let that thought fill your heart to overflowing. Let it invade the way you live, the way you talk, and yes, the way you golf.

⚐

Even so, come, Lord Jesus. Amen.

Phil Callaway with sons Jeffrey (left) and Stephen (right).

About the Author

When not working on his handicap, Phil writes books, speaks at golf tournaments, hangs out with his kids, and thinks about golf. He is the editor of Prairie Bible Institute's *Servant* magazine and the bestselling author of a dozen books including *I Used to Have Answers...Now I Have Kids, Making Life Rich Without Any Money,* and *Who Put My Life on Fast Forward?*

Described as "Dave Barry with a message," Callaway is a popular speaker at conferences, camps, marriage retreats, and Promise Keepers. He is a frequent guest on national radio and television, and he partners with Compassion, an international Christian child development agency. Phil's writings have won more than a dozen international awards and been translated into Spanish, Chinese, Portuguese, Indonesian, Polish, and English (one of which he speaks fluently). His five-part video series "The Big Picture" is being viewed in 80,000 churches worldwide. To find out about his other books or tapes, check out his website at www.philcallaway.com. For booking information, e-mail 3033@pbi.ab.ca.

Other Harvest House Books by Phil Callaway

Who Put My Life on Fast-Forward?

Pil Callaway shares his own stories and insights garnered from millionaires, CEOs, and "regular folk so tired they can hardly lace up their Velcro tennis shoes" to demonstrate how, with God's help, it's possible to start living deliberately in a high-speed culture.

Making Life Rich Without Any Money

With humor and candor, award-winning storyteller Phil Callaway shows readers how to find the happiness of a millionaire on the salary of a servant. Truly wealthy people enjoy laughter, simplicity, forgiveness and hope—whether they have money or not.

Parenting: Don't Try This at Home

In this sparkling collection of parenting-affirming stories, author and award-winning columnist Phil Callaway captures the amusing and bemusing experiences that tug at the heartstrings of anyone who's experienced the rollercoaster ride called "family." Phil turns sometimes-embarrassing moments into timeless spiritual lessons for young and old alike.